# TEACHING PRACTICAL CRITICISM

# TEACHING PRACTICAL CRITICISM

## AN INTRODUCTION

## MARGARET MATHIESON

CROOM HELM
London • Sydney • Dover, New Hampshire

©1985 M. Mathieson
Croom Helm Ltd, Provident House, Burrell Row,
Beckenham, Kent BR3 1AT
Croom Helm Australia Pty Ltd, First Floor,
139 King Street, Sydney, NSW 2001, Australia

British Library Cataloguing in Publication Data

Mathieson, Margaret
    Teaching practical criticism: an introduction.
    1. English literature—Study and teaching
    (Secondary)—Great Britain
    I. Title
    820'.7'1241   PR51.G7

    ISBN 0-7099-3504-8

Croom Helm, 51 Washington Street, Dover,
New Hampshire 03820, USA

Library of Congress Cataloging in Publication Data

Mathieson, Margaret.
    Teaching Practical Criticism.

    Bibliography: p.
    Includes indexes.
    1. English literature—study and teaching.
2. American literature—study and teaching.
3. Criticism—study and teaching. I. Title.
PR33.M38   1985     820'.7     85-3772
ISBN 0-7099-3504-8

302364

Printed and bound in Great Britain
by Billing & Sons Limited, Worcester.

# CONTENTS

Acknowledgements
Introduction

1.  PRACTICAL CRITICISM RECONSIDERED                          1

2.  THE 'NEW' SIXTH FORMER AND THE
    EXAMINATION                                              14

3.  EXPERIENCES OF ENGLISH 11-16                             32

4.  EASING THE PACE. SOME SUGGESTIONS                        50

5.  APPROACHES TO POEMS                                      71

    1.  'Snake'            D.H. Lawrence                      73

    2.  'November'              Ted Hughes                    85

    3.  'Ode on Melancholy'    John Keats                     96

    4.  'A Valediction:
        forbidding mourning'  John Donne                    103

6.  APPROACHES TO PROSE                                     112

    Childhood

    A Portrait of the Artist
    as a Young Man        James Joyce                       117

    Huckleberry Finn          Mark Twain                    121

    David Copperfield    Charles Dickens                    126

    Cider with Rosie          Laurie Lee                    129

Contents

### Weather

A High Wind in Jamaica     Richard Hughes     133

The Nigger of the
'Narcissus'     Joseph Conrad     137

### People

The Bostonians     Henry James     143

Middlemarch     George Eliot     147

Bibliography     153
Name Index     155
Subject Index     157

# ACKNOWLEDGEMENTS

For permission to use copyright material in this
book, the author and publishers wish to thank the
following:

Faber and Faber Ltd., for 'November' by Ted Hughes,
from Selected Poems 1957-1967;

The executors of the James Joyce Estate and Jonathan
Cape Ltd. for an extract from A Portrait of the
Artist as a Young Man by James Joyce;

The Hogarth Press Ltd. for an extract from Cider
with Rosie by Laurie Lee;

The Literary Estate of Richard Hughes and Chatto
and Windus for an extract from A High Wind in
Jamaica.

INTRODUCTION

Paper 3 Practical Criticism (2½ hours) (100 marks)
Two questions will be set, one calling for a comparison of passages, the other dealing with a
single passage.
                    English (Literature) Advanced Level
                    The Associated Examining Board 1984


On June 8, 1887, Edward A. Freeman wrote, in an
abusive letter to The Times, 'There are many things
fit for a man's personal study which are not fit
for University examinations. One of these is
"literature" ... it "cultivates the taste, educates
the sympathies, enlarges the mind". Excellent
results against which no one has a word to say.
Only we cannot examine in tastes and sympathies.'
Freeman, and his fellow dons who opposed the introduction of a School of English at Oxford, claimed
to fear the development of the study of literature
into the cramming of facts. Whilst it is likely
that they viewed the new subject's threat to the
supremacy of Classical studies even more anxiously,
it has to be acknowledged that the issues these
scholars contested so bitterly raised important
questions that continue to be very difficult to
answer. Today, when English is firmly established
in secondary schools and higher education, many
thoughtful commentators express dissatisfaction
with Ordinary and Advanced level examinations,
especially with the compulsory practical criticism
paper. Anthony Adams writes, in Sixth Sense, 'As
a method of increasing students' awareness of
the literary process, it (close critical reading
of literature) is admirable; as an examination,
ill conceived.'(1) Roger Knight says in 'Practical
Criticism Examined', an article which discusses

examination rubrics and examiners' reports, that
the exercise is 'inherently unsuitable for most
of the people who do it, that the instructions
tend to invite ... banalities and desperate evasions.
... In asking for a "critical appreciation" examiners were seeking an "analytical appraisal".' (2)
   No writer, therefore, offers English teachers
a book about the practical criticism paper without
misgivings. Candidates are asked, under examination
conditions, to engage in the difficult exercise
of expressing personal responses to literature
which demonstrate their ability to employ appropriate tools of critical analysis. It is a demand
which raises the central question of what it means
to study literature when we are still deeply confused about the relationship between affective
response and cognitive knowledge in English. It is
probably true that to discontinue this examination
could mean the disappearance from some classrooms
of a highly valued critical activity. It is certainly true that to offer alternatives to the
written critical response - opportunities for pupils
to show appreciation and understanding by reading
aloud, by discussing passages with examiners, by
writing 'creatively' - would produce severe admin-
istrative and assessment difficulties. Many commentators, however, believe that the uncertainties
surrounding the practical criticism paper in its
current form are sufficiently great for all of
these changes to be given serious consideration.
They believe that examiners underestimate the
problems which the examination produces for teachers
and that teachers frequently underestimate the
problems which their approaches to it produce for
their pupils. In a recent study which attempts to
redefine the nature of a literary education James
Gribble makes a convincing case for the value of
the critical activity and against its premature
introduction into pupils' and students' experiences
at school and university.

> If a critic is to do justice to the organic
> quality of works of art then he will require a
> highly agile and flexible mode of discourse to
> articulate it. We may be wary of introducing
> our students to such a mode of discourse prior
> to a wide acquaintance with works of literature
> since there are dangers of developing a facile
> slickness which skates over the surface of a
> work or straitjackets it in technicalities ...
> When literature and art become examinable

'subjects' there is often a tendency to count-
erfeit responses to works of art or even
simply to copy or ape the accounts which are
offered by teachers and text books.(3)

However deep and widespread commentators' dissatisfaction with current attempts to 'examine
tastes and sympathies' they agree that this examination is unlikely to disappear. Teachers, therefore, have to find ways of giving pupils confidence
in their ability to perform successfully on it.
Because I believe that many pupils lack confidence
about what is expected of them I have undertaken
two tasks: to examine the examination, in order to
discover the special problems it might produce for
contemporary sixth formers; to suggest some
approaches which teachers might take to prepare
pupils for the examination. By making proposals for
ways to teach inexperienced pupils to read literature with personal involvement and some attention
to simple technical matters I am aware of entering
a highly contentious area of English. What appears
to be a modest aim conceals, it might be argued,
both considerable arrogance, and considerable
ignorance of what many excellent teachers are
already doing. By making no proposals either for a
radically different examination or for ways in
which  teachers might draw upon the new disciplines,
linguistics and stylistics, I shall be seen merely
to be supporting the status quo. My defence is that
I believe this examination is likely to continue in
its current form, in the face of varieties of disapproval, and that I am anxious to disseminate more
widely some examples of helpful current classroom
practice which busy teachers have few opportunities
to publicise outside the classroom, except, very
occasionally, at their professional conferences.
My suggestions are based upon the trial and
error of classroom work with post graduates in
training and discussions with their teacher tutors.
They draw, additionally, upon observations and
recommendations made by investigators who have
undertaken research in this area during the past
twenty years. Since I am concerned with pupils'
transition from Ordinary level English and CSE to
the Advanced level literature course, and with what
might be the special difficulties of the 'new' sixth
formers, I am centrally interested in how balance
might be achieved between what pupils bring to the
texts and the direction and guidance they can be
given by their teachers. Reader response theorists

are currently urging critics and teachers to consider not just the authors and the texts but the
interaction taking place between the literature and
its recipients. 'All stories and poems are, after
all, explicitly or implicitly, addressed to an
audience, whose presence is as variable and problem-
atic as the storyteller's and poet's ... It is
the convergence of the text and reader', we are reminded, 'which brings the literary work into
existence.'(4) Pupils and students, like mature
readers, bring their previous experiences - of
living, and of reading texts - to every new text.
    More immediately and acutely than reader
response theorists, however, teachers of inexperienced young readers face the problem of controlling
and directing uncontrolled subjectivity. To encourage pupils' personal engagement with literary texts
teachers need to find ways of eliciting their
individual expectations, associations and special
interests. To discourage misreadings and unjustified
prejudices they need to find, not only initially
strong personal readings of their own, but strategies which anticipate and take account of their
pupils' ignorance and inexperience. Research conducted into pupil and student responses to complex
texts continues to confirm I.A. Richards' pioneer-
ing work in this area. Achievement of reading
maturity, it is agreed, is mainly a matter of
receptivity to the 'meaning of an author whose mind
is not coloured by the same presupposition as his
(the student's) own, or even to avoid importing
into a given text ideas from without'.(5) A group
of Advanced level English teachers in Wiltshire
who met recently to grapple with the problem of how
to define and teach 'style' quickly found themselves
faced with the diversity of their own and their
pupils' responses to selected texts. Their chair-
man's comments on one pupil's written response to
the poem 'Not My Best Side' by U.A. Fanthorpe raise
the question of the balance which teachers seek.
She writes:

> In this particular piece, Julie has made a
> very promising start, but as she develops her
> thoughts about the damsel in distress, it
> becomes clear that she is allowing the meaning
> that she brings to the poem to impose itself
> at the expense of the meaning implicit in the
> poem itself.(6)

# Introduction

Most teachers do not need to be reminded of
their responsibility to arrive at personal readings
of the texts and to guide and inform their pupils.
Their greater need appears to be for approaches
and strategies which increase pupils' confidence in
their own abilities to make sense of what they read
and to make discoveries worth sharing and developing. In the lower sixth, especially, teachers might
give direction from a less didactic stance than
many feel compelled to adopt and try to encourage
reciprocity between their pupils and the texts. In
this area of teaching Louise Rosenblatt's early
work continues to be relevant. Rosenblatt first
proposed the term 'transaction' to designate the
relationship between reader and text. She argues,
in <u>Literature as Exploration</u>, that 'the adolescent
needs to encounter literature for which he possesses
the intellectual, emotional and experiential equipment. He, too, must draw upon his past experiences
with life and language as the new materials out
of which to shape the new experience symbolised on
the page.'(7) Claiming that knowledge of literary
forms is empty without accompanying humanity, she
suggests that teachers try to involve pupils in
writers' concerns in order to set up a reciprocal
relationship with the texts.

> The young readers' personal involvement in a
> work will generate greater sensitivity to its
> imagery, style and structure; this in turn will
> enhance his understanding of its human impli-
> cations. A reciprocal process emerges, in which
> growth in human understanding and literary
> sophistication sustain and nourish one another.
> Both kinds of growth are essential if the
> student is to develop the insight and the skill
> needed for participation in increasingly com-
> plex and significant literary works.(8)

I hope that teachers and pupils will find to
be sensible the choice of poems and prose passages
I have made in my attempt to describe different
kinds of guidance which might be given in the classroom. I have chosen pieces which I observe are
frequently presented in class for 'practical criticism'. Each, as I explain in the discussion material,
introduces a variety of decisions for teachers who
are preparing lessons on them - about pupils' likely
associations with the 'subject matter', about their
readability, and about 'features of style' with
which pupils might become acquainted during class

discussion. The suggested approaches include both teacher directed and pupil initiated activities and, of course, try to integrate the affective and personal with the cognitive and technical in ways which might help candidates to cope with the demands of the examination. The practical sections of the book encourage English teachers to consider three factors in their preparation of practical criticism classes: pupils' likely experience and knowledge which can be related to the selected poetry and prose; pupils' likely difficulties with the material, anticipation of which might help them to make a personal response to the text; ways of introducing pupils to some very simple 'features of style', that is, the choice and arrangement of language through which writers recreate experience.

NOTES

1.   Anthony Adams and Ted Hopkin, Sixth Sense - Alternatives in Education 16-19 English: A Case Study (Blackie, London, 1980), p. 95.
2.   Roger Knight, 'Practical Criticism Examined', English in Education, 17, 3 (Autumn 1983).
3.   James Gribble, Literary Education : a Revaluation (Cambridge University Press, 1983) pp. 39-40.
4.   Wolfgang Iser, quoted by Susan Suleiman, The Reader in the Text (Princeton University Press, Princeton, 1980) p. 22.
5.   Ronald Morris, Towards Reading Maturity (Penguin Books Ltd., Harmondsworth, 1973) p. 97.
6.   Pat D'Arcy, Laurence Thirlway, Tim Noble, 'In Search of Style', Learning about Learning, Booklet No. 8, p. 13.
7.   Louise M. Rosenblatt, Literature as Exploration (Heinemann, London, 1970) p. 26.
8.   Ibid., p. 53.

Chapter One

PRACTICAL CRITICISM RECONSIDERED

This chapter identifies Advanced level English,
especially practical criticism, on the map of
English studies in universities and secondary
schools. It suggests that, although changes are
being proposed, or have already taken place, inside
and outside the sixth form - in undergraduate
studies, in English for younger pupils and in a
variety of alternative syllabuses, including
Advanced level Language - literary studies there
remain largely unaltered and passionately defended.
Although these changes are making it increasingly
difficult for some teachers to commit themselves to
Advanced level literature in its current form, they
appear, so far, to have failed to weaken the resolve
of the majority of examiners who control pupils'
experiences in the sixth form. Their view is aptly
summarised in a passage from the <u>Bullock Report</u>
which describes the aims of English teaching as
follows:

> In Britain the tradition of literature teaching
> is one which aims at personal and moral growth,
> and in the last two decades this emphasis has
> grown. It is a soundly-based tradition, and,
> properly interpreted, is a powerful force in
> English teaching.(1)

Recently, however, the perceived threats from
recommended changes in literary study in undergraduate courses have come uncomfortably close to
the more or less sealed off area of Advanced level
English. Although the 1983 symposium published in
<u>The Times Higher Education Supplement</u>, 'Complete
Diversity - or Disarray', focused upon English in
universities, its opening paragraph introduced
warning notes for work in sixth forms; 'even the

most cursory glance at literary journals and new
critical books reveals that ... literary study has
undergone what amounts to a Copernican revolution.'(2) The contributor referred, of course, to
structuralism, post structuralism and the wide
variety of disciplines within these broad developments which have been transforming the field of
literary aesthetics in America and Europe during
the past twenty years. Courses in text grammars,
text reception, theory of speech acts, narratology,
modal logics, logic of fiction, the whole field of
literary semantics, are now established at many
American and continental universities.

Setting out to demystify literature and, as
they see it, to set its study on firmer theoretical
foundations, structuralists have been directing
critical attention from the author and what he
actually says, the text, to the structures - codes,
genres, conventions - which allowed him to say it.
Structuralists argue that everyone, speaker and
author, draws upon language which predates him
for his utterance and writing. Utterances and
writing are, therefore, less the product or creation
of the speaker and the author that he is the product
of the language available to him. Structuralist
theories have shifted many scholars' attention away
from traditional concerns about authors' 'intentions'
and 'meanings' to linguistic and stylistic analysis
and, recently, to the psychological and sociological
structures underlying the texts. Rejecting suggestions for reconciliation between the 'traditional'
and 'linguistic' approaches in the classroom, a
linguist points out to English teachers the sharp
differences between the two and argues for their
continued separation. Entering a continuing debate
in The Use of English, Madeleine Ferrar argues that
'they are separate and neither need have any bearing
upon the other'. She claims that:

> The traditional approach puts stress on the
> validity of the author's perception of the
> world and the aesthetic validity of the text,
> whereas linguists are interested in how
> literary artifacts work - i.e. function.
> Linguists approach the text as if it were a
> well-made (and complicated) thing (product);
> the traditionalists perceive it as a revealing,
> insightful art object, which has to be ex-
> perienced before it can be fully understood.
> The vitriolic reaction to the linguistic
> approach in The Use of English is, perhaps,

indicative of the difficulty of reconciling
these two, very different ways of coming to
terms with the text. It is my view, however,
that once it is recognised that there is no
basic incompatibility between them, then the
two can exist side by side in the teaching of
literature.(3)

As dissatisfied as the structuralists with
traditional notions of textual unity and wholeness,
and the view of the study of literature as a moral
quest, post structuralists, or deconstructionists,
are especially interested in the contradictions to
be discovered within the text itself which illustrate the author's hitherto unchallenged ideologies,
particularly as these concern class, gender and
race. Post structuralists, or deconstructionists,
are interested in the diversity and multiplicity
of possible meanings available to readers in the
act of responding to the texts. Their critical
investigations set out to uncover the omissions, the
inconsistencies and the contradictions of which
readers are aware but for which authors have not
accounted. Their theories, as they have affected
work in schools take us back to the delicate and
difficult matter of balancing teacher direction and
pupils' personal responses to the texts. A group of
Leicestershire teachers, encouraged to adapt post
structuralist theories to their Advanced level work
on Othello, claim considerable benefits for their
pupils over traditional approaches to the text.
They report as follows:

A more intellectually demanding experience
came in the form of role-play in which every
student was given a role from the play, roles
ranging from Othello to the Turkish navy.
Roles were distributed at random with the carefully formed and emphatic instruction that it
was not merely the role within the play that
was to be examined, but that the play was to
be viewed in its entirety from the point of
view of the role.... Quite fine points of
motivation, for instance, could be worked at
by sustained questioning. The curious movements
of the Turkish fleet, the Duke's precise
relationship with Othello prior to the action,
Desdemona's upbringing and the rights of
paternity and many other issues were raised
and, if not dealt with conclusively or ex-
haustively, they were quite fully explored

moving from the text to imaginative projection outside it and back to the text again. A kind of post-structuralist interest in the 'gaps' of a text was thus made real within an activated imaginative context which became increasingly plausible as more roles were interviewed. At a later stage telephone conversations between roles were engineered which heightened the original role-play effect and which afforded marvellous opportunities for the students to make very suggestive possible connections in relationships.(4)

Introducing cautionary notes into enthusiasm for these approaches, David Lodge says, in his lengthy review of two major books on deconstructionist theories, that 'presumably one cannot deconstruct meaning until one has learned to construct it; certainly all the major deconstructionists are men and women who have passed through the traditional liberal humanist education. Their work derives much of its force and energy from their inwardness and familiarity with the values and assumptions they call into question.'(5) Whatever his misgivings, though, emphasis in literary theory outside the schools has shifted from the author and the text to the language and structures of which they have come to be seen as the products. It has moved, too, from the activity of interpreting the authors' intentions, of demonstrating the organic unity of their creations, to discussion of what various readers construct during the reciprocal process of engagement with the texts.

Linguists and stylisticians claim to have put literary studies on firmer theoretical foundations. Deconstructionists claim that their inclusion of readers' constructions into literary studies has strengthened and enriched these studies with philosophical, sociological and psychological considerations. Rejecting charges of encouraging uncontrolled subjectivity, deconstructionists argue that disciplined reflection about readers' responses to texts is likely to bring us closer to an understanding of the nature of literary discourse.

In the same year as the symposium in <u>The Times Higher Education Supplement,</u> in which seven university teachers discussed the significance of these changes for undergraduate English, an English teacher observed in <u>The Use of English</u> how remote all this appeared from Advanced level English in most of the schools. Summarising recent proposals

for change in English studies at undergraduate
level, Brian Hollingworth challenges his fellow
teachers to become aware of what he views as some
of their sinister political implications. Whilst his
article is mainly concerned to reject the Marxist
view of literary studies which, he says, has emerged
from the structuralist and post structuralist debates, it includes expressions of serious anxiety
about the current isolation of most school examinations in literature.

> There is a crisis in the teaching of English
> Literature, and a strange aspect of this
> crisis is that it hardly yet causes a murmur
> in the secondary schools of England. Tertiary
> levels of education are riven by structuralist
> and post-structuralist debate; young Turks seek
> to overthrow the bastions of Leavisian ortho-
> doxy, ageing trendsetters of the fifties and
> sixties try to adapt to the vocabularies of
> linguistic analysis and the science of semi-
> otics: Literature courses in the schools go on
> much as usual, with arguments largely restric-
> ted to the choice of set books and the liberty
> of the school to govern its own examination
> syllabuses.
> Liberal humanism, in a fadedly respectable
> form, is still the prevailing orthodoxy in the
> schools. It is the individual and the indiv-
> idual life which counts. The question, in a
> form suitably tempered to the audience, is
> still the Lawrentian 'how to live' - the appeal
> of the teacher is still to personal experience
> and his hope is still to extend sympathy and
> develop the subtleties of individual conscious-
> ness. Or else there is no question at all.
> There is just the desire to plough through the
> syllabus because it's there - to notch up one
> more examination success by sterile, old-
> fashioned appeals to categories like character,
> plot, theme or image.(6)

Sixth form English, moreover, can become
isolated from work in the lower and middle forms of
the secondary school if teachers have responded to
recent pressures for changes in their activities
with younger pupils. At the same time as the
'Copernican revolution' is taking place in some
universities, many schools have introduced pupil
centred approaches to literature, pupil initiated
creative activities, greater emphasis upon oral

competence. Indeed it may be partly because so
many changes have been recommended and so many un-
resolved questions surround English in the junior
and middle school - consequences, perhaps, of
teachers' acceptance of less extreme forms of
structuralism - that some teachers continue to support Advanced level English in its current form.
Their appreciation of its continuity with their own
undergraduate studies and the apparent security it
offers may be greater than their enthusiasm for
examinations which have their origins in the educational and social change of the twenties and
thirties.

Practical criticism, the 'unseen' or 'appreciation' papers, are intended to engage candidates
in a complex personal and intellectual activity
which involves their whole beings. These papers represent examiners' and teachers' convictions about
the moral value of close, critical reading, a view
of the study of literature which, as developed by
F.R. Leavis in the twenties and thirties marked a
radical break with earlier approaches to literature
which were modelled on the study of the Classics.
The compulsory practical criticism papers testify
to the success of Cambridge English in penetrating
universities and schools in this country. They
illustrate how Leavis' redefinition of the study of
literature as an experience involving the whole
reader - emotional, moral and intellectual - has
resisted intellectual dissatisfaction at university
level and developments in schools brought about by
educational and social change. Commenting upon this
success, Francis Mulhern concluded that:

> By the end of the war, Scrutiny's vanguard
> campaign against the old regime had succeeded;
> within a further few years, the rebellious
> ideas of the thirties had become dominant in
> the teaching of English. The literary canons
> established by Leavis became highly influen-
> tial, his critical methods even more so; and
> the broad cultural themes of his journal
> became commonplaces of secondary education.
> Many accepted them literally and in their
> entirety; reformed or diluted, debased and
> syncretized, they became the faith of a whole
> profession, an inclusive version of things
> that no other school subject and few university
> disciplines even attempted to match.(7)

Analysts, critics and historians suggest that

this peculiarly English phenomenon of investing literary criticism with the power to improve the quality of individual life and to restore cultural health to the community took place because Leavis' redefinition of this activity met a variety of perceived needs in the period between the wars. Geoffrey Strickland adopts Perry Anderson's view that there was an 'absence of any intellectual activity concerned with "totality" in England', and refers readers to 'the consciously unambitious nature, in this respect, of British philosophy, economics and history'.(8) In literary criticism alone, as conceived by Leavis, the notion of totality took refuge. When philosophy became 'technical, a displacement occurred and literary criticism became ethical'. Exploring the same phenomenon, Francis Mulhern considers what he sees as the appealing egalitarianism of the 'disciplined intelligence' which is supremely valued by Cambridge English. He argues that this, together with its fiercely moral stance, attracted and united the newly mobile provincial intellectuals hitherto excluded from the ancient universities. Carrying Strickland's explanation into his discussion of the shifting social composition of English intellectual life Mulhern writes:

> This disturbance of the discursive universe
> was redoubled by the quickening social
> recomposition of the intelligentsia that
> inhabited it. The aggregate effect of the
> changing occupational structure of the economy,
> the long process of reform and expansion in
> education, and the economic and political
> crises of the inter-war period, was to weaken
> the old intellectual bloc, whose inner cohesion
> and general authority had rested on its ties of
> kinship and privileged social intercourse with
> a confident ruling class. The inter-war intel-
> ligentsia was, by contrast, divided by social
> origin and occupational position, by political
> and cultural allegiance - deprived, in every
> salient respect, of security.(9)

In his tribute to Leavis' achievements as critic and teacher, George Steiner focuses upon three central features of his work which go far towards explaining the strength of examiners' and teachers' commitment to practical criticism as a worthwhile activity. He remarks upon its demands upon the whole, the complete, reader.

To Leavis, the critic is the complete reader:
'the ideal critic is the ideal reader'. He
realises to the full the experience given in
the words of the poet or the novelist. He aims
at complete responsiveness, at a kind of poised
vulnerability of consciousness in the encounter
with the text. He proceeds with an attention
which is close and stringent, yet also pro-
visional and at all times susceptible to revaluation. Judgement arises from response: it
does not initiate it....
  The critic's aim is, first, to realise as
sensitively and completely as possible this or
that which claims his attention; and a certain
valuing is implicit in the realising. As he
matures in experience of the new thing he also
asks, explicitly and implicitly: 'Where does
this come? How does it stand in relation to
...? How relatively important does it seem?'
And the organisation into which it settles as
a constituent in becoming 'placed' is an organisation of similarly 'placed' things, things
that have found their bearings with regard to
one another, and not a theoretical system or a
system determined by abstract considerations.(10)

The rest follows from this conviction about the engagement of the whole person, that is, that the
quality of the response reflects the moral quality
of the reader, and that to read with delicate discrimination means that one is fit to contribute in
a valuable way to the life of urban society. George
Steiner continues:

Such effort bears directly on the fortunes of
society. The commanding axiom in Leavis' life-
work is the conviction that there is a close
relation between a man's capacity to respond to
art and his general fitness for humane existence. That capacity  can be woken and enriched
by the critic. Literacy of feeling is a pre-
condition to sane judgement in human affairs:
'thinking about political and social matters
ought to be done by minds of some real literary
education, and done in an intellectual climate
informed by a vital literary culture'. Where
a society does not have within it a significant
contemporary literature and the parallel
exercise of critical challenge, 'the "mind"
(and mind included memory) is not fully alive'.

> In short, Leavis' conception of literary criti-
> cism is, above all else, a plea for a live,
> humane social order.(11)

Summarising what he believes to be the legacy
of Cambridge English, Francis Mulhern concludes
that it comprises three elements: 'a critical-
historical canon defining the major "traditions" of
English literature; a loosely formulated methodology
of critical practice, and a cluster of ideas con-
cerning the nature of literature and its place in
social life'.(12) Mulhern's critical stance, particularly on the 'loosely formulated methodology of
critical practice' is shared by George Watson, who
argues that much greater literary and historical
knowledge ought to be made available to students to
inform properly their literary judgements. He
believes that Cambridge English, with its high
valuation of the personal, the subjective, the
intuitive, has conspired with progressive educators' commitment to pupil and student centred
activities to encourage widespread anti-
intellectualism in our educational institutions. An
activity which allows literature to be 'a free play
area for personal judgement' and excludes any 'body
of knowledge' encourages readers, teachers and
critics 'not to know enough about anything' - or
care 'much for finding out'.(13)

As its assumptions have penetrated literature
teaching to younger pupils Cambridge English has
been held by some to be responsible for teachers'
unconscious elitism. Jeremy Mulford, writing about
his pupils' responses to a second rate poem, 'The
Snare', reflects upon the dangers of teaching
strategies which assume that there is a literary
critical 'right response'. He concedes that Leavis'
powerful influence is partly explained by the
appealing egalitarianism of 'the disciplined intelligence' which is intended to be independent of
social, cultural and intellectual privilege. He
goes on, however, to express anxieties about the
closures in lessons for which the teacher's concern about the 'right response' can be responsible.
His points, as we shall see, are relevant to much
that goes on in sixth forms, especially when we
consider the consequences of their recent dramatic
expansion.

> The influence - at least as much indirect as
> direct - of Leavis has been greater than it
> might have been because many teachers have,

paradoxically, used some of his ideas for what they see as egalitarian purposes. They have cut into the elitist logic and - rightly believing that a small minority of people does not have a monopoly of intelligence and sensitivity, and that literature should belong meaningfully to everyone - have done surgery on the obviously exclusivist parts. But in doing this they have usually failed to recognise the elitist base of the Leavisian model of the 'collaborative-creative process'. In fact, the very self-image of a teacher who sets out to eschew being a transmitter of culture in the crude sense, or who is not interested in fighting a rearguard action on behalf of traditional 'standards' or 'civilisation', can obscure the extent to which in trying to develop his pupils' sensitivity to a work or a body of works, he is merely trying to induce in them an approximation to his own 'sensitivity', an imitation of his own response. In that case, he is assuming an elitist position because the space he allows his pupils cannot but be too little to enable them to make what they can of what they have read.(14)

Despite widespread unease and uncertainty about the demands made upon candidates on the practical criticism papers it seems very unlikely that they will disappear from Advanced level English. Examiners and teachers, whatever their misgivings, remain too strongly attached to an activity which is intended to engage the whole reader, and to an examination which is meant to evaluate both personal and intellectual qualities, to abandon it for either 'creative' writing or objective analysis. Whilst it might seem reasonable, in view of the perceived value of creative writing in the junior and middle school to extend this into Advanced level English, few teachers trust themselves or examiners to assess this reliably at sixth form level. It is unlikely, moreover, in the present climate, that universities would accept evaluation of this ability as a means of selection of prospective undergraduates. It is equally unlikely that many examiners or English teachers will be attracted by an examination which assesses candidates' abilities to analyse texts in exclusively linguistic or stylistic terms. The pejorative tones of many examiners' reports upon candidates who provide evidence of mere technical knowledge do not encourage optimism about changes in that direction. Their dislike of this finds

strong support amongst the subject's opinion
leaders. In his critique of Patrick Doughty's
article, 'Linguistics and the Teaching of Literature', Fred Inglis maintains that the language
teacher in English has freed himself 'from anything
but technical training. His ignorance empties
language of its morality.'(15) Fear of the loss of
the personal, more importantly, the moral element,
in the displacement of practical criticism by linguistic analysis has produced a variety of expressions of resistance and hostility. Roger Knight,
detecting Burton and Carter's greater enthusiasm for
their models and jargon than the literature they are
discussing in <u>Literary Text and Language Study</u>, is
especially severe about their dismissal of the
'personal' in the reading process. He says that:

> No literary critic could accept the simple
> pejorative implication of that 'personal' as
> against the assumed objectivity of some scheme
> of formal analysis. He knows that it is not in
> the nature of judgement in this field that it
> can be 'interpretable with respect to objective
> analysis'. Good literary criticism arises out
> of a disciplined subjectivity; being moral in
> nature it can have no other source.(16)

Thus, in however imperfect a fashion it is
offered and assessed, the practical criticism paper
seems likely to survive the hostility, dissatisfaction and difficulties it creates. Its strengths
derive from examiners' and teachers' high valuation
of the total, the whole, the integrated response.
Its critics, whatever their arguments' merits about
disguised elitism, absence of scholarship and
pupils' despair and confusion, threaten to displace
it with exercises judged likely to exacerbate the
perceived fragmentation within the curriculum and
wider society. Resistance to the introduction of
linguistics and stylistics to replace the individual,
personal, intuitive responses currently invited by
this examination derives currently from four main
sources: linguists' lack of interest in the personal
and moral elements; their disregard for the social,
historical and literary uses of language; the
threatened proliferation of disciplines likely to
fragment literary studies into semantics, historical
linguistics, structural linguistics, stylistics,
etymology, philology and so forth; and its inevit-
able consequence, preoccupation with separate small
units, the word, phrase, sentence, the parts and

not the whole. Supporting Fred Inglis, Roger Knight, Philip Hobsbaum, Frank Whitehead, Peter Abbs and David Holbrook - graduates of the Cambridge School - in their stance against new, competing disciplines, Geoffrey Strickland writes, in his masterly critical review of recent developments:

> To understand what someone is saying is not a matter of understanding the words in isolation and the grammatical connections between them. It means also understanding the interest and importance for the writer and speaker of what is written or said, distinguishing between the cry for help made in jest and the same cry - that is, the same words - uttered in genuine fear.(17)

Although practical criticism continues to be well defended, it seems likely that many English teachers' confidence in its value has been badly shaken by persistent expressions of hostility by university scholars. Unhelpfully, however, the new university disciplines, like the 'new' grammar from which so much was hoped, have failed to provide either persuasive arguments or accessible language yet to support alternative approaches to the study of literature in schools. Meanwhile, teachers and pupils have to prepare for an examination in practical criticism which is intended to assess the quality, as defined by Cambridge English, of candidates' responses to literature. It is with the special difficulties which this creates that the next two chapters will be concerned.

NOTES

1. A Language for Life, (HMSO, London, 1975) p. 125.
2. The Times Higher Education Supplement 11.2.83., p. 12.
3. Madeleine Ferrar, 'Linguistics and the Literary Text', The Use of English 35/2, Spring 1984, p. 39.
4. Gerry Elmer and Nick Peim, 'Othello: A Drama Approach to 'A' Level English', Drama and Dance, 3, 3, Summer 1984, p. 85.
5. David Lodge, 'Books about books about books', The Times Education Supplement, 22.4.83, p. 15.
6. Brian Hollingworth, 'Crisis in English Teaching', The Use of English, 34/2, Spring 1983, p. 3.

7.  Francis Mulhern, The Moment of Scrutiny (NLB, London, 1979) p. 319.

8.  Geoffrey Strickland, Structuralism or Criticism (Cambridge University Press 1981) p. 156.

9.  Mulhern, The Moment of Scrutiny, p. 312.

10.  George Steiner, Language and Silence (Faber, London, 1967) p. 250.

11.  Ibid., p. 251.

12.  Mulhern, The Moment of Scrutiny, p. 328.

13.  George Watson, The Discipline of English (The Macmillan Press Ltd., London and Basingstoke, 1978) p. 9.

14.  Jeremy Mulford, 'Comments on traditions of literature teaching', a shortened version of 'Afterword' in an unpublished report Children as Readers: The Role of Literature in the Primary and Secondary Schools, cosponsored by N.A.T.E. and the Schools Council 1968-73.

15.  Fred Inglis, 'How to do Things with Words' Language Study in English Lessons.

16.  Roger Knight, review of Literary Text and Language Study, R. Canter and D. Burton (eds), Arnold, 1982, The Use of English, 33/3, p. 61.

17.  Strickland, Structuralism or Criticism, p. 90.

Chapter Two

THE 'NEW' SIXTH FORMER AND THE EXAMINATION

The purpose of this chapter is fourfold. It is to
describe briefly the context inside which many
English teachers are currently working at Advanced
level in schools and colleges, that is, the likely
composition of their classes and their pupils'
aspirations. It is to survey Advanced level examiners' demands upon candidates in the practical
criticism paper during recent years. It is to
review examiners' opinions of candidates' performances on this paper. Lastly, it is to consider some
of the strategies apparently taken by many teachers
in this area as well as those recommended in the
most popular course books. The chapter suggests that
the coincidence of changes in the composition of
most Advanced level groups during the past twenty
years and the persistence of the compulsory practical criticism paper appears to have created difficulties for many teachers and their pupils; 'poor
performance in The Unseen', Peet and Robinson
assert, 'is the greatest single reason for failure
among Advanced level candidates'.(1) Additionally,
it develops the view taken in the last chapter that
this examination is surrounded by uncertainties as
to its purpose and criteria for success.
     Today's sixth form is no longer a small elite
group concentrating upon Advanced level subjects to
prepare for entrance to further education and
training. The traditional grammar school began to
come under pressure in the fifties and sixties, its
average size in maintained schools trebling in less
than twenty years. Whereas in 1952 the majority of
sixth formers taking Advanced level examinations
entered universities, this was no longer so in 1969.
Pupils began to enter the sixth form at the end of
the sixties to meet employers' demands for Advanced
level passes to train for managerial positions and

because, in a period of increased prosperity, more
parents were prepared for an extra two, if not five,
years beyond compulsory education to give their
children greater occupational opportunities. Since
then, sixth form numbers have continued to grow and
its membership to diversify. Today the situation
remains similar to that analysed in the Schools
Council Working Paper 45, 16-19: <u>Growth and Res-
ponse</u>, January, 1970.

> Approximately
> > 75 out of 100 are 'traditional' sixth
> > formers following A-level courses;
> > 3 out of 100 are 'traditional' sixth
> > formers following post O-level courses
> > but not A-level ones;
> > 25 out of 100 are 'non-traditional' sixth
> > formers not following any post A-level
> > courses.
>
> Of the total population of this age group in
> the schools in 1970 of 184,000 about 12,000
> from the first group, 5000 from the second
> group, and 40,000 from the third group - a
> total of 57,000 - leave after the first year.
> In the case of the second and third groups this
> is nearly all of them. We should add to this
> the fact that of those pursuing a three-subject
> A-level course, nearly a third can expect to
> fail or to secure a pass in no more than one
> subject.

Unsurprisingly the number of candidates taking Maths
and English rose especially sharply within this
overall increase. Between 1966 and 1977, the number
taking English rose from 45,000 to 58,860, girls
continuing to outnumber boys by a ratio of 3:2, an
important factor in any consideration of the examination, since fewer girls than boys intended to
continue  into higher education. Along with Maths,
English remains one of the most popular Advanced
level subject but, dominated by girls, is less
likely to be perceived as a preliminary to undergraduate study.

The aspirations and likely destinations of
pupils in many Advanced level English groups are
very varied. The dedication and motivation recalled
by commentators on the 'new' sixth form as characteristics of their contemporaries at school is
likely to be found in only a minority of English
groups. English now tends to be the third subject
taken by pupils more interested in other courses.

15

Adams and Hopkin say that 'it is seen very often as
having a specific utilitarian value in aiding
effective communication; it is a favourite subject
beyond O-level for those staying in the sixth form
for one year but who have no intention of proceeding
to university or any form of higher education'. In a
large comprehensive school or sixth form college
there appear to be three broad categories of Advanced level pupil taking English now. There are
those keenly interested in continuing into higher
education to specialise in English at BA and BEd
level, possibly half the total population entered
for the examination. Secondly, there are those also
hoping to enter higher education for whom English
is a second or third choice. Thirdly, there are
those joining an Advanced course, highly likely to
be English, either because a pass at this level is
necessary for their chosen training or for whom
occupation has to be found whilst they retake
Ordinary level examinations or prepare for one year
qualifying examinations in other subjects. Speaking
at a NATE conference in 1968 Boris Ford wistfully
compared the contemporary sixth form with his own:

> I think one can identify a number of important
> factual changes (in the composition of the
> sixth form)
>
> a.   A change from a small select authoritative
>      group of twenty or thirty to large classes
>      within a total sixth of perhaps two hund-
>      red, often with no sixth form room (I
>      shared a study with one other boy)
>
> b.   A change from a university orientated
>      group, many of them doing work of an almost
>      first year university calibre under a First
>      Class Honours man, to a large group orient-
>      ated towards higher education at large,
>      doing varieties of work under teachers less
>      able than the best of themselves.

In Sixth Sense, published in 1981, Anthony Adams and
Ted Hopkin introduced similar recollections though
with considerably less enthusiasm. To support the
central argument of their book, which is for the
development of more appropriate courses for new
sixth formers, they point out that:

> the A level of 1970, and of 1980, has in most
> cases remained substantially unchanged since

its introduction in 1951 and that was sub-
stantially the same in content, though different in structure, from the Higher School
Certificate that had preceded it. But both
these examinations were designed to fit into a
tripartite school system; they were essentially
grammar school examinations and, in consequence, the setters of syllabuses and the
examinations were able to make a series of
assumptions about the population at which they
are aimed.(2)

In spite of the changes which have taken place and
their consequences for the Advanced level study of
English, few serious attempts have been made to
revise the examinations. In spite of the high
failure rate on the examination as a whole and, it
appears, on practical criticism particularly, most
of the boards remain attached to the compulsory
inclusion of this component. Many examiners and
teachers share a powerful conviction about the
special value of the criticism paper both for its
beneficial effect on  sixth form teaching and as a
means of assessing candidates' abilities to respond
sensitively to literature. They appear unconvinced
by arguments about the essential elitism of the
exercise or expressions of uncertainty by English
scholars and educationists about the precise aims
of this part of the examination. They appear
unshaken by annual evidence of many candidates'
severe difficulties upon being asked to express in
a very brief period, under examination conditions,
their personal responses to the selected passages.
Indeed it seems likely that resistance to criticism
of this paper may have hardened as the numbers
taking English at Advanced level have increased and
the quality of many candidates' critical powers is
perceived as unsatisfactory. Within the tradition
whose supporters view the ability to read literature
with critical discrimination as evidence of highly
valued personal qualities, the loss of this exercise
at Advanced level would be deeply regretted.
Believing, as many do, that these qualities will
be developed by their preparation for the examinations and that they can be assessed in candidates'
answers, they are likely to remain unwilling to
abandon it for a course which would be restricted
to the set books. For many English specialists in
schools and universities practical criticism is
their subject's central activity. In their view it
is, therefore, highly desirable that all pupils

become engaged in it, most especially since the
examination is not intended to favour the culturally
advantaged, the technically well prepared or the
candidates who have been thoroughly rehearsed on
their set texts. No recent critics of the practical
criticism paper are optimistic about the possibilities of its disappearance from the Advanced level
English examinations.

What follows now is a representative selection
from the major Advanced level boards' demands upon
candidates in the paper variously called practical
criticism, critical appreciation and comment, and
comprehension and appreciation. Except for the
Oxford and Cambridge local examinations and a few
of the currently available alternatives at Advanced
level, this is a compulsory element on papers, or a
separate compulsory paper of two and a half hours
which carries a fifth or a third of the total
available marks.

The University of Cambridge, 1982, (Critical
Appreciation and Comment) asks candidates to choose
two out of three questions which are firstly on two
poems, secondly on two prose passages and thirdly
on either a poem or a prose passage. Candidates are
instructed to:

1. Write a critical comparison of the following two poems. You should pay attention to
   differences and similarities in content,
   style and feeling, saying what you take to
   be the main characteristics of each poem.
                    or
2. Write a critical appraisal of the two
   passages, paying particular attention to
   the evocation of mood and ways of looking
   at a landscape.
                    or
3. Write a critical essay on either the poem or
   the prose passage printed below.

The University of London, 1983, (Comprehension
and Appreciation) asks candidates to choose two
questions from unseen drama, poetry and prose, the
first of which, the drama, being compulsory. On the
front page of the paper candidates are told that
'either favourable or adverse comment on the
selected passages is equally welcome, provided that
you cite ample evidence from the texts in support of
your views'. On the drama candidates are asked:

to discuss the passage as a piece of writing

> from a play, paying particular attention to the
> use of language and the way ideas are devel-
> oped.

On the poem they are asked:

> to write a careful study ... paying attention
> to such matters as subject, style and total
> impression, and indicating whether you like
> it or not.

On the extract from a novel candidates are asked
three directed questions calling for 'analysis',
'overall impression' and 'contrast' of parts within
the passage.
    The Southern Universities Joint Board, 1981,
(Paper 3) instruct candidates to answer both
questions set. Firstly they ask them to:

> Read the poem and write a critical appreciation
> of it.

Secondly, on the poem and then on a prose passage,
they are asked to:

> Read the prose passage and write a critical
> appreciation of it, making any points of
> comparison with the poem that seem helpful.

    Northern Universities Joint Matriculation
Board which, in its course description of Advanced
level papers, asks pupils to give evidence of their
ability to 'use ... critical powers on unseen
passages of verse and prose' and for this to be
demonstrated on two passages in the available time,
asks them to:

> 1. Compare and contrast the following poems,
>    commenting on such aspects as the way each
>    poet treats the subject, his use of
>    language and his handling of verse form.

On the two prose passages set in 1981 the examiners
asked the following, more directed questions:

> 2. From the pen portrait of the characters,
>    how is the reader prepared for their
>    entry from the author's use of irony and
>    contrast. Illustrate your answers in
>    detail.

# The 'New' Sixth Former and the Examination

The Welsh Joint Education Committee also asks for two answers on their two and a half hour examination. The following instructions are given:

1. Write a detailed appreciation of one of the following poems, making reference to its theme, its presentation and response to the poem as a whole.

2. On the prose extract: write a detailed critical appreciation of the following passage, considering in particular the effect the author creates, the means he uses to that end and your response to the passage as a whole.

Clearly the Boards agree about what constitute the important features of an exercise in practical criticism. The selected passages of drama, prose and poetry are intended to be read either for the first time, or to have been encountered previously only outside the set books. They hope that all candidates' sixth form experiences of English will have prepared them to read new material carefully, with personal involvement – that is, being ready to approve or disapprove of it – and have equipped them with appropriate critical tools to explain writers' intentions and effects to justify their judgements, that is, by referring to such matters as theme, subject, style, language. Examiners are all interested in candidates being 'critical', in Cambridge's 'critical commentary' and 'critical appraisal', JMB's interest in evidence of 'critical powers', Southern Universities' 'critical appreciation' and Welsh Joint Education Committee's 'detailed critical appreciation'. For most boards it is highly desirable, if not explicitly stated, that candidates should be prepared to communicate their own views, their 'response to the poem as a whole' and demonstrate the 'full play of their sensibility'.

Boards differ in what appear to be minor matters, although, as critics of this examination argue, the language in which these differences are expressed indicates several important uncertainties about aims of the exercise. There are variations in the difficulty of the task set and thus, possibly, in the amount of depth expected in candidates' answers. Opinions are divided about whether attention should be given to a single poem or prose passage, or to two, between which comparisons and preferences are invited. There are considerable differences, also, in the phrasing of directions to candidates. The questions themselves fall into four broad categories: the non directive (write a critical appreciation of the following); the lightly directive (compare and contrast the following poems, commenting on such aspects as the way each poet treats the subject, the use of language, and his handling of verse form); the more specific (write a critical evaluation of the following poem, referring to such matters as theme, feeling and tone, verse form and imagery); and the heavily directive (read the following ... and answer the questions which follow). Across the boards candidates may be asked to attend to any of the following features of a poem: feeling, sense, meaning, verse, verse forms, structure, style, thought.

This account of the factors which might explain why practical criticism 'is the paper which is responsible for most candidates' failure at Advanced level' continues with a survey of examiners' opinions of many candidates' performances. Their annual dissatisfaction appears to outweigh heavily their pleasure. One can only be impressed by the power of the boards' convictions about the examinations' advantages in the face of disappointing responses by the majority of their candidates. Examiners' reports generally make depressing reading, partly because of the inexperience and panic which candidates' answers have shown and partly because their expressions of dissatisfaction are so often vague, inconsistent and unhelpful, especially on the matter of critical terminology.

AEB who introduced this examination very recently reported after its first year as follows:

> Most candidates wrote very badly, and many who did so seemed far from unintelligent. Worthy, caring candidates after worthy, caring candidates simply did not know how to set about the practical criticism of short literary texts. This emerged no matter which passages were chosen and, one suspects, would have emerged no matter what passages were set ... Few candidates have much sense of the discipline of practical criticism, that they must respond only to the words on the page.
>
> (AEB Examiners' Report, 1979)

On points needing particular attention AEB complain that many candidates 'did little more than

paraphrase'; 'too many speculated wildly', or used
the passages as springboards for essays on other
subjects or 'the riding of hobby horses'. The invitation to give 'your response to the passage as a
whole' was too often met by 'a torrent of tedious
waffle that was either sentimental praise or mind-
less abuse, or intimate accounts of the effect of
reading upon the reader'. In the following year
AEB examiners, conceding that there had been some
improvement, nevertheless reported that 'disturb-
ingly it remains obvious that some candidates do
not prepare at all and enter the examination room
ignorant of the demands of critical appreciation'.

Most boards regret Advanced level candidates'
poor understanding of what they read, especially
poetry. The following comments illustrate examiners'
perennial disappointment, even disbelief, about
many candidates' failure to show evidence of having
understood what the passages were about. They had
either been unable to transfer their helpful classroom experiences to new material in the examination
or had been given insufficient help to understand
what they were intended to do.

> It is over that matter of the understanding
> of the poems that most doubts may be expressed
> ... it was believed that substantially the
> subject and development of each poem was
> straightforward; the rubric instruction sug-
> gested the main areas for comment ... Scores
> of candidates launched straight away into extra-
> vagant discussions of the punctuation of the
> poems ...
>
> (JMB 1981)

Noticeably the following comment points up some of
the variations in criteria and terminology employed
in this examination; 'understanding' has been
replaced by 'experience', whilst 'subject' and
'development' by 'tone, mood and feeling', arguably
quite distinct rather than interchangeable features.

> There was, in some cases, simply not enough
> attention paid to the experience of the poem,
> to its tone, mood and feeling which need to
> be responded to if the poem is to be fully
> understood and appreciated. Failure to do
> this led to failure to grasp the meaning,
> leading to an inability to maintain a con-
> sistent and logical argument.
>
> (JMB 1981)

Examiners discover each year that many candidates cannot give written evidence of having read literature with detailed attention, of having understood the purpose of authors' selection and arrangement of language, of having 'appreciated' (or of giving evidence of being equipped with the appropriate tools to express this appreciation) the variously termed 'experience', 'tone', 'mood' and 'feeling'. They are unhappy, moreover, both about the irrelevant and, often, eccentric answers of those who have not tried to please them and the likely insincerity of those who have. Illustrating the examiners' tendency to identify performance on practical criticism with the candidates' moral qualities one board insists:

> There is also need for more honesty on the part of the candidates. They must not feel that passages always have to be praised with a mindless and gushing insincerity. The work of many would be improved if they had the confidence to move from analysis and description to considered evaluation.
>
> (AEB 1982)

Setting aside the problem of distinctions between analysis and evaluation, examiners' introduction of 'honesty', 'sincerity' and 'confidence' raise anxieties about the subjective element which inevitably enters assessment in this area.

Critics of practical criticism on the Advanced level examination argue that candidates' problems of trying to express a 'personal response' (often to material deliberately chosen for its unfamiliarity) are compounded by the examiners' own uncertainties about the function of critical terminology. Sometimes examiners create severe difficulties for candidates by appearing to want expressions of personal response and objective analysis simultaneously, a forbidding demand on young readers. They ask for evidence of candidates' ability to refer to 'matters as theme, feeling and tone, verse and imagery' on the one hand, and to attempt a 'critical valuation' or a 'personal response' on the other. Roger Knight quotes extensively from the Cambridge Examiners' Report, 1978, to illustrate his disquiet. This is what they say they wanted:

> What should have been noted was Coleridge's account of the nightingale's song which he both suggests and imitates by his choice of

words, his phrasing and by onomatopoeia. By
his phrasing Coleridge imitates the short
bursts of song which work up into a crescendo
and to a long sustained note. The sound and
sense echo each other throughout. The vocabulary with its combination of conversational
tone and poetic diction ('tis the merry night-
ingale', 'disturbance', 'inhabits not') its
success in capturing the bird's song ('fast
thick warble', 'with skirmish and capricious
passaging', 'murmurs musical and swift jug
jug') and with also its signs of addiction to
the Romantic ('delicious', 'sweet') should
also have been commented on in detail.

The examiners' specific comments on the scripts they
reproduced, Knight argues, strongly suggest that
'the favoured candidate is the one who is able to
produce a pedestrian catalogue of such effects even
though he shows no greater awareness of the nature
of the poem: conversely, a candidate who demon-
strates such awareness will incur disapproval if he
fails explicitly to note the effects the examiners'
list. Of one such candidate it is said that "he
writes an 'appreciation' to some extent but not a
'critical' one". "Critical" here clearly means
analytical of the surface features of the poem; it
is a narrow use of the word that can only encourage
what elsewhere the Cambridge examiners have dis-
missed as "irrelevant technical analysis".'(3)
    The formidable difficulties of achieving an
acceptable balance in an area where the examiners
themselves reveal uncertainties must be discouraging
to many teachers and pupils. Whilst it is true that
most examiners expressed reservations have been
about candidates' misuse of critical terminology,
there is evidence to suggest that some examiners,
some years, are unhappy about its appearance at all
in candidates' answers. Indeed, they sometimes give
the impression that candidates who employ critical
terminology are failing to engage with the material
in an emotionally sincere way. In 1981 JMB com-
plained about candidates' inclusion of 'loads of
learned lumber' in their comparison of two sonnets
about Shakespeare by Milton and Arnold. Whilst the
examiners acknowledged that 'technical terms and
stylistic qualities had been thoroughly taught',
they added 'perhaps overtaught' to indicate their
discontent.
    In-service discussions and post-graduate
seminars about preparing sixth formers for the

practical criticism paper annually illustrate wide-spread uncertainty on this issue. Many teachers are bewildered by the conflicting messages from the boards about the employment of critical terminology expected from their candidates. The following extract from an investigation into this problem by a post-graduate student during ten weeks' teaching practice at a sixth form college summarises well many teachers' uncertainties:

> Teachers could be forgiven for concluding that there are two but mutually contradictory views which they should hold on this issue: that candidates should be discouraged from using terminology since at this stage of their development it is usually a sign of a funda-mental failure of response; that students should be introduced systematically, over their sixth form experience, to certain crit-ical terms so that they are able to integrate them effectively into the language available to them for the discussion and written expres-sion of their experience of reading. The compromise view, and the one that in practice presumably holds sway, is that students should 'discover' these terms only when they them-selves appreciate their usefulness, and in this way instances of irrelevant usage or the suppression or avoidance of 'genuine response' will diminish. Ideally, this results in the acquisition of literary terms in the context of particular experiences of reading; the experien-tial and the technical are thus less likely to lose contact with each other in a manner which encourages us 'to hide our genuine responses behind clever manipulation of received vocab-ulary, notions and approaches'.(4)

This summary of a trainee teacher's impressions of the problem leads into the final section of this chapter which sets out to describe some of the approaches taken by teachers and prescriptive writers to practical criticism. There is no research evidence available in this country about what takes place in Advanced level classrooms, which means that impressions can be drawn only from examiners' reports, one's own and post graduates' observations and recommendations made in course books.

Some pupils, examiners are convinced, are given no preparation for the criticism paper. In 1979 and 1980 AEB and Welsh Joint Committee agreed,

though they express their views in slightly different ways, that 'some candidates do not prepare at
all and enter the examination room ignorant of the
demands of critical appreciation'. It seems very
likely that some English teachers, from conviction,
out of frustration, or fatigue, do leave their
pupils to manage as best they can on this paper,
hoping that the close reading of the set books will
prepare them sufficiently well for the exercise.
Much will depend upon the generosity of the time-
table, the availability of committed, confident
specialists and their ability to resolve the uncertainties surrounding the rubrics, the questions
and the examiners' reports.

From the Reports, and from tutors' and students' observations of sixth form classes and
discussions with staff, preparation appears to fall
into two broad categories for many pupils. The
first, apparently 'open' approach, is often taken
by academically highly qualified teachers whose
contribution to English in the school is their very
successful work with the most promising, often
culturally advantaged pupils. They introduce their
whole groups, however, to a wide range of literature
outside the set books during their sixth form course
and tend to treat the material in the same way for
everyone. Passages are given out with instructions
to prepare comments, or distributed to be read as
unseens at the beginning of a lesson. Few conces-
sions are made to historical, literary and technical
ignorance out of perceived respect for the student's
individual response, and likely resentment of 'spoon
feeding'. The discussion is approached by way of
open questions: What do you make of it? What is the
tone of this poem? In response to often very perceptive contributions expressed by students rated
'good at English', university potential, teachers
tend to engage in dialogues with their most confident pupils or to talk themselves about the poet,
the intricacies of a tricky section, interesting
likely interpretations and so forth. In this way
critical terms are gradually introduced for employment in later exercises and gradually, it is hoped,
confidence grows in their appropriate employment.
The danger with this 'inspirational' approach is
that often only the most able pupil will acquire a
repertoire of terms which can be used with concept-
ual clarity. The rest, often stimulated, sometimes
discouraged and bemused, will be left with a few of
the more easily remembered technical terms which
they employ in a desperate fashion in examinations

in order to give their unsure responses some kind of support.

As this approach can be questioned for its occasional disregard for the 'average' and 'below average' candidate, who is often simply less confident, because less culturally advantaged and successful in conventional ways, so can the very different strategy which emphasises knowledge instead of response, or experience. Many teachers, it seems, take highly structured, systematic approaches to practical criticism. Pupils are given notes on historical, cultural and literary background, glossaries of critical terms and are taken through a course book designed to equip them to recognise form, features of style and a range of technical devices. Anxious, possibly, to compensate for what they fear have been too free, pupil centred, creative approaches in the middle school, and concerned about Advanced level successes for university aspirants, they approach the study of literature in a highly directed, technically rigorous fashion. It seems likely that this method will give the whole range of pupils greater confidence in tackling many of the apparent demands of the unseen; but unless matters of attitude and response have been included, pupils' answers seem to the examiners to be too 'mechanical'. Those candidates who appear, in the examiners' view, over-dependent upon technical analysis are criticised for describing rhyme schemes 'mechanically' and for listing 'figures of speech without indicating their effectiveness' (London, 1981). Whilst AEB regret many candidates' lack of an adequate critical vocabulary, they insist upon avoidance of what they call the 'computer-scan' or 'I spy' approach to criticism, concerned merely to note examples of stylistic effects. Many English teachers appear to find it very difficult to prepare a wide range of candidates to integrate the personal and emotional elements of the reading process with technical analysis of writers' craftsmanship.

Not surprisingly, in view of all the uncertainties surrounding practical criticism, much of the prescriptive writing tends to be unhelpful to inexperienced pupils. Organisation of course books varies widely; some consist of paragraphs, or fully illustrated essays, on critical terms; some give brief, often densely argued, introductions followed by extracts for practice; some integrate definitions of the critical experience with step by step explanations of features of style and recommended

approaches to commentary and response - one course
book includes pupils' essays of different quality
with critical comments. Many course books are char-
acterised by their likely difficulty for most
entrants to sixth form Advanced level groups and by
the tendency of the early ones, especially, to
mirror the vagueness of the examination itself about
the relationship sought between personal response
and critical analysis.

In 1953 H. Coombes says in his introduction to
Literature and Criticism, a text recommended to
English teachers by AEB in the eighties,

> real literary analysis has no affinities with
> grammatical sentence analysis. Its accuracy
> is not that of classification. It is that of a
> delicate discernment and assessment of the
> experience, of the 'felt life' ... in and
> behind the words that are being examined...
> A knowledge of the terms used in critical
> practice has nothing to do with keenly and
> freshly responding to a piece of writing.(5)

Emphasising that knowledge and appreciation of
critical terminology is no substitute for personal
qualities like discernment, keenness and freshness,
Coombes' purpose, nevertheless, is to take the
reader through features of style in order to intens-
ify and fortify his spontaneous sensitivity.
Curiously, for beginners, he opens with a consideration of rhythm and, more curiously, with examples
of unsuccessful attempts by writers to integrate
this with their central experiences. Swinburne,
pupils are told, 'is indulging in what may be
called poetical incantation', Dryden's 'words do not
carry any great sense of loss' and Poe 'establishes
his rhyme mechanically'. Although the chapter's
central concern is rhythm, it includes, without
explanation, alliteration, assonance, repetition,
onomatopoeia and punning. It has much in common
with the stimulating, often inspirational, sometimes
bewildering, lessons by English teachers determined
not to condescend to their sixth form pupils.

An experienced English teacher across a wider
ability range, Roger Harcourt, introduces features
of style very gradually in Sharing Literature.
Individual words, their significance in context,
rhythmic effects and complex associations are given
detailed discussion, full explanations and evaluation. Harcourt too invites, and makes clear he
highly values, personal engagement, insights and

opinions and does not disqualify his priorities by
moving too rapidly to complex analysis. He repeat-
edly refers to the importance of the young reader's
'individual response to literature', asking him to
'pit (his) sensitivity to language and (his) understanding of life against various artists ... the
premium is on involvement and understanding ...
there is no doubt that a sensitive and involved
response to poetry offers the best equipment with
which to face any examination'.(7) His book, in
common with many gifted teachers' lessons, opens
generously and persuasively about the importance
of individual, of personal response and continues
helpfully in its early discussion of technical
points. One wonders, though, what inexperienced
pupils make of the sections in which he expresses
preferences for one poem above another as some
examiners wish candidates to do on their papers. It
seems likely that this writer, gifted teachers and
the examiners have arrived at the stage when they
can discriminate - that is, condemn Stephens' 'The
Snare' for sentimentality, banality, the use of
language which fails to interest us, 'gushing,
simplistic and embarrassing' after many years'
experience of careful, tutored reading and that it
may be difficult for some pupils to concur, sin-
cerely, with their judgements. In his comparison of
Larkin's 'Myxomatosis' and Hughes' 'Thrushes'
Harcourt says of the second poem '... for all its
cleverness, the words are unmemorable. It isn't a
question of intelligence or sensitivity or interest
in language. It is more like a failure in poetic
response. The language has no reverberation, no pool
ripple effect, to catch the subtler issues of
experience; ploys of rhythm and diction strike us
merely as ploys.'(8) It seems unlikely that many
inexperienced readers can become sufficiently confident to evaluate literature in this way, that is,
to condemn a poem acknowledged as 'intelligent' and
'sensitive' for 'failure in poetic response' and for
rhythm and diction which are 'merely ploys'.

After a supportive, encouraging introduction
during which technical analysis is put briskly
into its secondary place, ('your writing should
have some personality') Peet and Robinson proceed to
explain and illustrate metres in detail unlikely
ever to be needed by Advanced level candidates.
Cowper's 'Poplars' is criticised for its 'jog-
trotting banality of rhythm and rhyme. The metre is
not exactly regular, in fact. All four lines are
tetrameters, but only in the second are all four

feet identical, each of the other three lines begins
with an iambic foot instead of an anapaest ...'.(9)
Most pupils taught in this fashion are likely to
think that they should produce similar technical
information under examination conditions, and thus
risk incurring their board's displeasure about
'learned lumber'.

Finally, there are course books simply too
difficult to give much help to struggling sixth
formers. After short, dense introductions assuming
unreasonable familiarity with the critical process,
they give a selection of extracts followed by even
more difficult questions than those on the papers
themselves. After Rupert Brook's 'The Dead', Ginger
asks pupils 'Has the poet succeeded in conveying as
a poetic experience the sense of living intensely
and enjoyably?' and to 'examine the syntax of the
poem. Does it help to reproduce a poetic experience?'(10) After reading 'Ode on a Grecian Urn'
pupils are asked 'to consider the relationship
between form and content'.(11)

Much, therefore, is unsatisfactory about the
practical criticism paper. Examiners and most prescriptive writers (12) fail to distinguish sufficiently clearly between the nature of the reading
process - the personal response - and its organisation in a written examination answer; they assume
too readily pupils' ability to subordinate critical
terminology to critical discrimination, that is, to
respond-and-analyse; they tend to be confused and
confusing about their demands for evidence of
pupils' ability to handle critical terminology. In
the following chapter I shall consider reasons
outside the practical criticism paper itself which
might further explain many pupils' difficulties
with this exercise.

NOTES

1.  Malcolm Peet and David Robinson, The
Critical Examination (Pergamon Press, Oxford,
1977), p. xii.
2.  Adams and Hopkin, Sixth Sense, pp. 9-10.
3.  Knight, 'Practical Criticism Examined'.
4.  Jan Todd, 'Sixth Form Literature and
Literary Theory', dissertation submitted for the
award of PGCE, University of Leicester, June, 1983.
5.  H. Coombes, Literature and Criticism
(Chatto and Windus, London 1953) pp. 13-16.
6.  Ibid., pp. 21-25.
7.  Roger Harcourt, Sharing Literature (Oliver

and Boyd, Edinburgh, 1975) p. 30.
    8.  Ibid., p. 28.
    9.  Peet and Robinson, The Critical Examination,
p. 29.
    10.  John Ginger, An Approach to Criticism
(Hodder and Stoughton, London, 1970) p. 45.
    11.  Ibid., p. 56.
    12.  Two recent publications suggest approaches
to Advanced level English which depart from the
traditional course books in this area: John Brown
and Terry Gifford, 'Creative Responses in the Sixth
Form, English Studies, 11-18, edited by Bernard
J. Harrison, (Hodder and Stoughton, 1983); David
Self, Critical and Creative (Harrap, London, 1984).

Chapter Three

EXPERIENCES OF ENGLISH 11-16

This chapter considers the major changes which have
been recommended to secondary English teachers
during the past thirty years and their likely consequences for pupils' readiness to cope with
practical criticism at Advanced level. It points out
that the generous optimistic spirit of these changes
is consistent with examiners' invitations to candidates to express their personal responses to
literature which were discussed in the last chapter.
It argues, however, that they may have contributed
to many candidates' difficulties in responding to
literature in the personal and analytical fashion
demanded by the examinations. Finally, it develops
an earlier suggestion that the issues raised in the
structuralist and post structuralist debates in the
universities may have seriously challenged some
young teachers' commitment to the practical criticism exercise.

It does not attempt to set English teachers'
problems against the context of cultural developments, especially in the media, during this period.
I.A. Richards, F.R. Leavis and Denys Thompson, Fred
Inglis, G.H. Bantock, George Steiner and many other
critics have written comprehensively about what they
view as the likely consequences of these for
teachers and pupils engaged with imaginative literature. Nor does it discuss the reorganisation of
secondary education and innovations in teaching and
examination strategies, except as they have in-
directly affected sixth form work in English. Its
main aim is to draw English teachers' attention to
the kind of problems which might have been produced
for their sixth formers by shifts in emphasis in
their subject from the texts to pupils' apparent
interests and needs, to indicate the likely mis-
match between what is expected from pupils on the

practical criticism paper and what many of them will
have experienced in English earlier in their
schools. It is generally acknowledged that today's
sixth formers are even less well prepared for the
technical demands of practical criticism than those
entered for Advanced level English in earlier gen-
erations. Sixth formers in the fifties and sixties
were likely to have been taught in smaller, more
homogeneous, academic groups than those entered for
English examinations today. Most of today's sixth
formers, almost all of whom are compelled to tackle
the practical criticism questions, do not enjoy that
advantage. Many, moreover, are likely to be even
less well informed than their predecessors about the
Classics, the Bible and historical background to a
variety of literary periods. Many are likely to be
hampered by their unfamiliarity with traditional
grammar - so far not replaced by any help from
linguistics and stylistics - their limited acquaint-
ance with literature outside this century and their
lack of experience of close reading in school which
was undertaken specifically to analyse, appreciate
and evaluate writers' craftsmanship. None of these
problems is new. Almost wholesale adoption of the
unseen paper by examination boards has merely exposed difficulties which have continuously beset the
study of literature by inexperienced readers.

This chapter does not argue for a return to
traditional examination papers and teaching methods.
I.A. Richards' examples of undergraduates' failures
in practical criticism show convincingly the lack
of success of traditional methods in encouraging
attentive and discriminating reading. Its purpose
is to prepare for suggestions made later in the
book for approaches which might give pupils greater
confidence than many appear to possess about
attempting practical criticism. The book's aim is
not to reverse current trends in English teaching.
It seeks teachers' sympathetic consideration of the
difficulties their sixth formers might currently
experience in practical criticism classes and
suggest ways of trying to meet and overcome them.
Additionally, it sets out to persuade them to extend
into the sixth form those approaches which have been
most successful in promoting younger pupils' personal involvement with literature.

The major changes prescribed for English
teaching since the Second World War are these: that
pupils should be encouraged to express their personal responses both to real life experiences and
to literature in their own poetry and prose, in

improvised drama and in small group and class discussion; that pupils should be encouraged to consider personal and public issues, emotional, social
and moral, in English lessons, to go beyond the text
to wider issues for debate and discussion; that
pupils should be given frequent opportunities for
talk in a variety of situations in order to improve
their linguistic competence. I shall consider each
of these developments separately.

During the past hundred years English as a
school subject has risen in status, broadened in
interpretation and taken on a powerful sense of
moral purpose. From its beginnings as two rudi-
mentary skills in the useful knowledge of the nineteenth century's elementary school curriculum
English has come to be regarded as 'coexistent with
life itself'. It has grown, especially since the
Second World War, to be the school subject viewed as
the major humanising experience in the curriculum,
with the pupil's creative response - as reader and
writer - at its centre. In 1969 a group of American
specialists who had spent a term observing classes
in seventy schools here selected for the quality of
their English departments identified teachers' aims
in the following passage:

> The teaching of English in British schools is
> the teaching of creative response. Involvement
> in the creative act seems to be the primary
> goal ... Feeling and doing, not knowing, are
> the central concerns. While the end product of
> the American educational system is the critic,
> the end product of the emerging British system
> is the artist.(1)

As discussed and proposed in contemporary prescriptive writing, creative English aims to elicit
pupils' personal responses to literature and to
experience. It seeks to involve the whole child by
appealing to his feelings, both about the books he
reads and his relationships with the outside world.
Literature and situations in everyday life are
selected for their likely power to arouse strong
feelings, the expression of which is encouraged in
class discussion, dramatisations and personal
writing. Personal involvement is perceived as the
beginning of an imaginative process which will
engage the whole child when it finds expression in
his creative writing. Most especially from younger
pupils, English teachers ask for poetry and prose
stimulated by their responses to works of mature

writers and to events in their own lives. Many teachers blame traditional examinations in English for diminishing opportunities to continue this work throughout the school, claiming that children's creative potential is destroyed by examinations' emphasis upon their <u>knowledge</u>, rather than <u>experience</u> of literature, and by demands for writing in outworn and inappropriate models. Keenly interested in the uniqueness of every pupil, Edmond Holmes, a leading figure in progressive English during its early years, gave his strong support to children's writing in schools, arguing that composition is central to the growth of individuality. Anticipating David Holbrook, who asks for English teachers to promote pupils' 'real revelation of self' in creative expression, Holmes says:

> I mean by composition, the sincere expression in language of the child's genuine thoughts and feelings. The effort to express himself (in language) tends, in proportion as it is sincere and strong, to give breadth, depth and complexity to the child's thoughts and feelings and through the development of these to weave his experiences into the tissue of his life.(2)

Drawing heavily upon Wordsworth of <u>The Prelude</u> and Coleridge's definitions and distinctions in <u>Biographia Literaria</u>, Marjorie Hourd argues, in <u>Education of the Poetic Spirit</u>, that English teachers should encourage the essential creativity in each one of us; to do so is truly to accommodate the growing mind. She suggests that, in their early years, children should explore the nature of self and of personal relationships through dramatic enactment of episodes from ballads and myths. She proposes that, throughout their years at school, all pupils should be encouraged to order their responses to experience through prose and poetry writing. Conceding that 'all children are not poets in words', she says, however, that 'many more of them are poets than we think, and our job as teachers is to leave the way open'. James Britton supports creative writing in his postscript to <u>The Eye of Innocence</u>, a volume of children's work, because it involves pupils' feelings in a classroom activity and thus is likely to heal some of the divisiveness experienced in the outside world. He argues:

> The highly personal creation of the artist ... comes as near as anything can to representing

> the unique individual, the person, the unit in
> the network of human relationships, the 'I'
> that reacts to experience, acts and suffers and
> learns and goes on.(3)

As the concept of wholeness gained official
acceptance in educational thought in England, increasing prominence has been given both to the role
of imaginative literature and to children's creative
achievements. In English, above all, it has been
persistently argued, it should be possible to engage
the whole child in his experiences at school and
thus to combat the destructive effects of the fragmentation of the outside world. This view of English
and the arts has been forcefully expressed by prescriptive writers from Edmond Holmes to David
Holbrook, perhaps most powerfully by Herbert Read in
his highly influential book, <u>Education through Art</u>.
Read asserts in this volume that

> the purpose of education, as of art, should be
> to preserve the organic wholeness of man and
> his mental faculties, so that as he passes
> from childhood to manhood, from savagery to
> civilisation, he nevertheless retains the unity
> of consciousness which is the only source of
> harmony and individual happiness.(4)

Gradually these views have penetrated prescriptive writing about English teaching in secondary
schools. The persistent efforts of supporters of
creative English, especially David Holbrook and
Peter Abbs, have brought about a shift of emphasis
in examinations and teaching methods from the texts
to pupils' responses. GCE and CSE candidates are
asked to express their personal responses to unseen
passages of prose and poetry and invited to describe
their reactions and give their opinions in answers
about characters, incidents and moods in the boards'
selected literature. It is now customary to find the
following information in the rubric for a Mode 3
Literature folio: 'original writing in response to
literature may account for up to three of the minimum of ten major pieces'. Much of the course work
for this examination, therefore, consists of pupils'
short stories, scenes and poems stimulated by literature as evidence of their personally felt understanding which is preferred by many teachers to
regurgitation of plots and technical analysis of
style. The Cambridge Plain Texts Ordinary Level
paper also illustrates this preference in its

questions on the set books and the optional unseen poem. On the conversations between Orsino and Viola in Twelfth Night, Act Two, scene four, it asked, in 1980: Some people find this one of the most interesting and appealing scenes of the play? What do you see in it? On Julius Caesar it asks: Portia says of herself 'I have a man's mind, but a woman's might'. What problems does Portia have to face? How will she cope with them, do you think? On Lord of the Flies, candidates were asked: How do you feel towards Samneric?; and about Jack and Piggy: Whose side would you take, or do you find yourself wanting to stay neutral? And the optional question upon Seamus Heaney's 'The Forge' illustrates official changes in emphasis from exclusive knowledge about the text to inclusion of the pupil's personal response. After pointing out several of the poem's features, the question continues: When you have got to know the poem well in this way, write down the thoughts and feelings it stirs in you; do this in whatever way seems to you best - there is no 'right' method or opinion.

Prescriptive writers, examiners and, on the evidence of conferences and contributions to journals, many committed English teachers, share enthusiasm for pupil centred, creative approaches to literature. They share the wish to avoid setting remote and inaccessible texts and asking for facts about plots and characters as well as technical examination of form, metre, rhyme and imagery which, many believe, discourages immediate sincere response to the material. From the first form, where pupils are invited, after reading 'Spit Nolan' or 'Hawk Roosting', to give accounts of similar experiences or descriptions of pets, to CSE and GCE, emphasis tends to be placed upon enjoyment and involvement, and oral and written evidence sought of personal engagement in the writers' subject matter. And for as long as we remain centrally interested in making literature enjoyable and in the pupils' 'real revelation of self' in their personal writing, the benefits of these approaches are likely to have been impressive. The difficulties, however, arise from the current uneasy coexistence of these approaches with demands at Advanced level, and even GCE, that pupils give evidence of their ability to combine their personally felt responses with analysis of writers' intentions and craftsmanship. It has become hard for pupils to believe that it is their sincere response which examiners seek when they ask also for evidence of analytical skills dependent upon confidence in close, objective and informed reading of the material.

The second recommended change in approach to English in secondary school which is likely to have affected pupils' readiness for the close study of literature is from the consideration of complete texts to extracts arranged around themes and topics. This has taken place against the broad background of official acceptance of progressive educational theories as they have influenced school and classroom organisation, the curriculum, teaching strategies and methods of assessment. The shift to comprehensive schooling and mixed ability teaching encouraged the movement away from remote and inaccessible texts to topics judged more relevant to a wide range of pupils who could tackle them on their different levels privately, and co-operate publicly in projects, discussions and drama. The accompanying shift to the pupil's activities from the text and the teacher encouraged problem based learning which, it was hoped, would stimulate pupils to enquire of adults, libraries and other resources and move outwards from the literature into wider social and moral issues. If themes and topics, supported by interesting extracts from prose, poetry and drama seemed directly relevant to pupils' lives, the effect would be not only to promote enjoyment of literature and to prove its close relationship with the real world, but to demonstrate its links with other parts of the curriculum. Additionally, thematic approaches offered new freedoms to teachers normally dictated to by examination boards to choose their own material, make their own resources and, in the case of Mode III CSE, be their pupils' examiners.

Two educational trends in particular encouraged this movement away from the study of a wide range of complete texts to extracts drawn from mainly contemporary writing grouped around topics and themes. Firstly there was growing enthusiasm for integrated, or interdisciplinary, approaches to learning in the arts subjects. Educators' anxiety about the loss of a liberalising subject in the school curriculum when the Classics and Religious Education declined in importance led them to move English, at first, into the character building role of the older subjects. In the late sixties many English teachers were urged to co-operate with historians, geographers and social scientists, especially, to devise work for average and below average adolescents, to take thematic approaches to learning. The

Humanities Project's goals, to 'encourage tolerance
and the ability to think humbly' and to 'assist the
development of a capacity to make value judgements
which are based on more than prejudice' were to be
achieved by way of plentiful classroom discussion
stimulated by a variety of material relevant to a
controversial issue. To these ends the traditional
authority of the teacher and the texts was to give
way to pupils' opinions, reactions and enquiries.

> Our strategy must renounce the position of
> teacher as 'expert', capable of solving by
> authority all issues about values that arise in
> discussion - because the position cannot be
> logically justified. Yet it must be discip-
> lined, so that the teacher understands his
> purely procedural authority in the classroom -
> his authority as 'chairman' and can maintain
> it. Teaching must be based on discussion and
> enquiry.(5)

It seems likely that the shift encouraged by supporters of Humanities from the text to the pupil's
perceived needs and interests has had consequences
for Advanced Level literature similar to those produced by the move to 'creative' English. It has
meant that teachers and pupils in the middle years
have been mainly concerned with the subject matter
of the material and that this has been deliberately
chosen for its power to provoke strong feelings and
expression of these in debate and discussion. The
following introduction to a Humanities Course in the
sixties illustrates teachers' enthusiastic commitment to pupil centred approaches to the selected
literature.

> The Humanities Course aims to give you an
> opportunity to discover more about yourself and
> the world of people in which you live. It is
> intended to increase your awareness of other
> people's experiences and of your own - of
> beliefs, thoughts, attitudes and relationships.
> It is to give you a chance to explore your
> feelings, to express your ideas and to create
> your own version of the world which you
> find.(6)

The excited, spontaneous immediacy of the best of
these lessons which are intended to provoke an
exchange of opinions in class - thus satisfying
notions of enjoyment, activity, participation and

egalitarianism - as well as many teachers' deliberate avoidance of detailed attention to the texts, is
captured in the American visitors' comment in their
chapter on this work. 'Every class', they say 'was
a kind of happening ... Everything was geared to
feeling, not knowing.'(7)

The other educational movement which directed
English teaching away from the authority of texts
and teachers into theme and topic based learning -
away, consequently from 'knowing' in the sense of
organisation and style, and away from literature as
complete texts and from periods outside this century
- was the radicalism of the early seventies. The
'New Left' urged teachers to dismantle texts and
rearrange them around issues judged relevant to contemporary pupils. Many young teachers during this
period accepted the perspective of cultural relativ-
ism as it appears in books like Nell Keddie's
Tinker, Tailor, John Holt's The Underachieving
School, in Postman and Weingartner's Teaching as a
Subversive Activity. The school, they argue, should
accommodate and encourage working class children's
culture, instead of imposing what they see as an
alien, middle class curriculum upon them. From this
standpoint, insistence upon the value of great
literature represents endorsement of middle class
values. Radicals in English teaching, who wish to
promote working class and coloured children's confidence and pride, attack exclusive concentration
upon literature because, they argue, this supports
and perpetuates the established social system. They
believe that teachers can bring pupils to self ful-
filment and improve their quality of life in wider
society by making English work against the social
system which the school supports rather than within
it. As the influence of this criticism of traditional English affected some classrooms it combined
with the efforts of Humanities supporters to separate literature into extracts illustrative of
important contemporary issues. Pupil directed
discussion, ideally again about contentious topics
on which teachers have no 'expert' information, was
proposed by the radicals to increase children's
confidence by challenging the traditional view of
their teachers' knowledge and control. Radical
teachers were, and perhaps still are, bitterly
critical of much that goes on in schools, even in
progressive teachers' classrooms, on the grounds
that it assumes the goal of making 'children more
like teachers'. Standards of correctness, they
claim, are nothing more than evidence of social

convention and prejudice too long responsible for the discouragement, even humiliation, of working class children, along with the literature of the 'alien, middle class curriculum'. The following statement illustrates the radicals' perspective on these changes:

> Liberal English is more than a pedagogic idea; it is a political one ... it is wrong to speak of a 'change in teaching method' when a moment's reflection persuades us that what we are involved in is nothing less than a revolution in the English classroom and to a lesser extent within the total institution we work in.(8)

Thus far this chapter has been concerned to point out the widening gap between many pupils' experiences of English in the early and middle years of secondary school and the demands still made upon them at Advanced level. It suggests that pupil centred approaches taken for either artistic-creative or social reasons are likely to contribute to candidates' difficulty with unseen complex literature to which they are expected to respond both emotionally and intellectually. Little wonder that whilst many feel confident to make a 'personal' response, they are unlikely, unless sensitively prepared, to combine this with discussion of features such as writer's subject matter organisation and 'style'. Many would be far better equipped by their earlier experiences to produce a piece of personal writing or comments on the moral and social implication of the subject matter.

Their difficulties with writer's meaning and style is unlikely to have been lessened by the implications for English of the third major shift in emphasis. Closely linked with the ideas underpinning the Humanities Programme and radical English supporters' topic-based English are those expressed by educators recommending a change from the written to the spoken word in the classroom. They are united in the urgency of their recommendations by a sense of social injustice. Knowledge that 'a tiny percentage of the population has been given access to the principles of intellectual change, whereas the rest have been denied such access', has led to proposals about teachers' changed attitudes towards working class speech being made as if it is upon these that greater social justice depends. The tone is set by the <u>Newsom Report</u>.

> The overriding aim of English teaching must be
> the personal development of the pupil. And of
> all the different aspects of English, speech
> has by far the most significant contribution to
> make towards that development.(9)

Supporters of oral work share the Humanities'
Project's assumption about our need to consider an
education which takes account of change. Both
express concern about pupils' capacity to survive in
what they see as society's state of flux; it rests,
they claim, upon pupils' increased range of linguistic control and ability to confront controversial
issues. Rigidity in teachers' approach to questions
of value and standards in language use limits
pupils' capacity to cope with the changing world
outside school. Unless they abandon the notions
of 'correctness' and 'right and wrong' answers, they
will be failing to provide education which is a
preparation for life. Harold Rosen insists upon the
central role of language acquisition in teachers'
efforts to achieve pupils' survival in a changing
world as well as greater social justice.

> If we have a climate of continuous change in
> society, then the struggle to make meanings out
> of a continuous flux of our experience demands
> an ability to perform rapidly and successfully
> a whole range of symbol exchanges ... As
> language plays so central a part in the auto-
> nomy and operational effectiveness of individ-
> ual human beings, then their capacity for
> survival is seriously affected, in so far as
> they find themselves continuously in a situ-
> ation where their attempts to make sense of new
> experiences are frustrated by their lack of the
> necessary language for learning a language for
> living.(10)

Teachers have been asked, therefore, by Denis
Lawton, James Britton, Harold Rosen and Douglas
Barnes to exchange notions of correctness for
'appropriateness' as befits a range of social situations. They have been asked to talk less themselves
and to let their pupils talk more. To extend the
range of their linguistic repertoire pupils should
be asked to give directions, give instructions, take
part in simulated interviews, tell their fellow
pupils about personal experiences, work out problems
in group discussions and take part in improvised
drama.

Plentiful evidence exists of the extent to which pupils benefit from these activities. Teachers comment very favourably upon the introduction of oral assessment in CSE, reporting how previously un-motivated pupils have become more willing to talk about their interests and to work in a lively, en-gaged fashion. One's regret is that few pupils appear to be given opportunities to develop these skills in their Advanced level literature courses. If teachers could find ways of employing similar strategies in the sixth form to create pupils' engagement with literary texts, developments in this area of English might be viewed as wholly beneficial. If, however, oral work is discontinued in the sixth form, and if it has deflected teachers' and pupils' attention away from writing skills lower down the school, it might be seen as a contributory factor in pupils' unreadiness for the demands of the Advanced level course.

Very few pupils, it appears, either because of teachers' unfamiliarity with grammatical terms, uncertainty about the value of 'doing grammar' or convictions about its deliberate exclusion, will know, when they enter the sixth form, the conven-tional grammatical terms for parts of speech, phrases and clauses and sentence structures. Such knowledge is no longer tested by Ordinary level examinations. Its general neglect affects only the practical criticism paper at Advanced level on which, as we have seen, examiners ask for evidence of close reading which includes discussion of 'features of style'. Teachers, therefore, need to find ways of giving help of some kind if pupils are to be expected to comment upon the effects of writers' organisation of language with any confid-ence. It might be simply a matter of discovering whether the terms of formal grammar are familiar and, if not, deciding upon the value of introducing them. It might mean limiting enquiries, in the early stages, to observations about long and short, simple and complicated, sentences. The main point is to avoid assumption of knowledge and experience which is not available to pupils on entry to the sixth form.

As long as English teachers support the criti-cism paper they need to consider the nature and organisation of the guidance their pupils require. Chapter four makes a series of proposals which take account of most pupils' inexperience with its demands, and Chapters five and six apply these to selected poetry and prose. Their aim is to seek

pupils' personal involvement in literature, that is,
to retain the strength of child centred approaches
to learning, and also to introduce questions of
writers' craftsmanship. Ways are suggested of introducing material, directing reading, and analysing
texts which might sharpen pupils' powers of appreciation and increase their confidence in their
abilities to respond to literature at this level.

The major problems surrounding this exercise,
which arise from changed cultural conditions and
uncertainties at every level about the study of
English will persist, however, to challenge every
teacher of Advanced level pupils. Their pupils'
likely ignorance of the Bible, the Classics and
historical background means that teachers must
decide afresh how much information to give ahead,
during or after, the first reading of every text.
This decision should feature as a major part of
lesson preparation. It cannot be dealt with by a
mere warning such as Peet and Robinson give in their
brief reference to 'semantic change'. If this is
ignored, they point out, students 'often make dreadful mistakes when, for example, paraphrasing or
interpreting the word 'presently' in a Shakespeare
play or the word 'enthusiasm' in an extract from
Swift, or by misunderstanding the complexities of
meaning present in a word like 'nature' as it was
understood by Pope or Wordsworth'.(11) An investigation into college students' problems with T.S.
Eliot's poetry revealed that in addition to the
difficulties already discussed - sidestepping into
issues provoked by the subject matter - they were
seriously penalised by their ignorance of Biblical,
classical and historical allusions. After detailed
analysis of transcripts which demonstrate the
students' confusion, the investigation concludes
that 'it was evident that (they) had little or no
access to those sources of meaning which could have
enriched their understanding of the themes of the
poem'.(12) In his essay which challenges nineteenth
century optimism about the power of the humanities,
especially poetry, to humanise individuals and
societies, George Steiner notes the inaccessibility
of much vernacular literature to today's well
educated adult readers. The classical references in
the two extracts from Shakespeare which he discusses
'would have been eloquent to an Augustan with any
serious claim to literacy, to a Victorian public
school boy, to much of the educated European and
English bourgeoisie, until, say 1914'. Today, he
says, footnotes lengthen, glossaries become more

elementary, and 'poetry loses immediate impact'.(13)
Steiner's discussion of undergraduates' difficulties with literature of the past raises the first
of two important points to be considered about
English teachers themselves who are preparing pupils
for the practical criticism papers. They, like
today's sixth form pupils, may be very different
from the honours graduates teaching small groups of
highly motivated pupils during the period when
critical discrimination was introduced into Advanced
level English. They may be less broadly and deeply
educated than their predecessors, either because
they come from less supportive cultural backgrounds
or because they have experienced differently composed undergraduate courses. Colin McCabe, arguing
for a radically changed approach to undergraduate
English studies, supports George Steiner's view
about the likely remoteness of many texts currently
included in most conventional university courses.

> The possibility of undertaking a course which
> will cover English literature from Chaucer to
> the present day is now so manifestly absurd
> that it astonishes me that claims that such a
> course can be taught are not routinely met with
> howls of derision. How do you teach courses on
> English literature to students who know nothing
> of Christianity? What is the point of asking
> students to read a piece of discursive prose
> from the sixteenth or seventeenth century when
> the current dominance of spoken forms of the
> language, particularly on television, means
> that sentences of any complexity are simply
> perceived as unreadable?(14)

Charting cultural and educational changes since 1945
Francis Mulhern raises similar questions about many
teachers' intellectual preparation for adopting the
critical strategies introduced by Cambridge English.
Arguing that 'twin cultural movements, discursive
and social', brought Scrutiny into being and then
carried it away, Mulhern claims that the decade
after the Second World War was decisive for their
development.

> 1945 was not only the year in which Butler's
> meritocratic educational reforms began to take
> effect; it also saw the emergence of the first
> whole generation of teachers of English trained
> in the spirit of 'the critical revolution' -
> a generation deeply influenced by Richards and

> Leavis but relatively lacking in the inter-
> disciplinary competence that had produced their
> innovations and sustained them in practical
> form.(15)

Of equal importance, as they are likely to undermine
consensus among English teachers about the need to
encourage and practise critical discrimination, are
the uncertainties raised by the structuralist and
post-structuralist debates in the universities. As
these debates have already affected work in the
schools by questioning the authority of literary
texts, many English teachers have enthusiastically
accepted the shift to oral work for average and
below average children and the integration of
literature into thematic work judged more relevant
to the lives of the majority of pupils. In many
schools these changed approaches coexist with conventional lessons in the sixth form based upon traditional assumptions about the civilising influence
of great writers. Not all teachers, however, find it
easy to resolve these contradictions.

Some young teachers are likely to have had
their convictions about the authority and significance of literature challenged during their university courses. Some will have been encouraged to
adopt a relativist, perhaps Marxist, stance which
they are eager to take into the schools. As Brian
Hollingworth says, in 'Crisis in English Teaching'
the structuralist debate has serious consequences
for the committed teaching of English inside the
theoretical framework of liberal humanism. Firstly,
it threatens teachers' sense of the special value of
literature and, equally serious for the 'critical'
exercise, it questions the basis upon which judgements between writers can be made.

> Structuralist arguments seem to conflict with
> the confident orthodoxies of English teachers
> in many ways. They question whether literature
> can be differentiated by value from other forms
> of writing; they question whether it is meaning-
> ful to try to discover the intention of the
> author in writing his work - or even to discover the
> author; they question whether literature is
> actually saying anything at all about 'life' in
> the sense that most readers unsophistically
> understand it. But more fundamentally, they can
> question the ideology which has traditionally
> informed the study of literature - the very
> idea that such a study is a 'humane' activity.

The theory of value on which structuralist arguments rests is relativistic. Basically, since the observation of human societies suggests to us that values are not permanent entities - that what is valued by one civilisation or one historical epoch is not necessarily valued by another - it seems reasonable to infer that value lies in the eye of the beholder and, by extension, to argue that one set of values cannot be demonstrably better than another.(16)

Hollingworth continues by suggesting that many young teachers are likely to be deeply worried about reinforcing, through their teaching, an unjust, manipulative society. Like Francis Mulhern, who analyses the demise of Cambridge English partly in terms of its political conservatism, Hollingworth argues that many key figures in university English today - Terence Hawkes, Terence Eagleton, Catherine Belsey, Peter Widdowson - have bitterly criticised its contribution to cultural domination. Many are taking a Marxist perspective which urges the study of literature as a means of production instead of exclusive concentration upon the texts themselves. Terence Hawkes argues as follows:

What strikes me as a much more valuable pursuit would require a slight shift of focus. It would require us to confront, not the 'great' works of art in themselves but the ways in which those works of art have been processed, produced, presented, worked upon, in our own time and previously, as part of the struggle for cultural meaning outlined above.
This will inevitably involve a deep commitment to the study of theories of criticism. In this form 'English' would consist not of a supposedly innocent encounter with literary texts but of an analysis of the ways in which the meanings of those texts are produced.
This is another way of saying that we should teach our students that texts are texts. As such, given our system of education, they constitute highly significant and sensitive areas in which competing forces within our culture struggle for domination.(17)

Although Hollingworth disagrees with this view, on the grounds that 'the basis of good teaching is

questioning rather than inculcation', he acknow-
ledges that 'the challenge which such theories
represent and the crisis which faces English studies
should not be underestimated'. For many leading
figures in English, educators' current preoccupation
with pupils' linguistic competence, together with
radicals' enthusiasm for Humanities has produced a
deeply unsatisfactory situation throughout the
school. Frank Whitehead, David Holbrook and Peter
Abbs, lamenting what they view as a return to a 'new
utilitarianism', or 'disintegrated studies', claim
that English has lost its way, and that there is a
failure of confidence in English. 'Once', David
Holbrook says in English for Meaning, 'there was a
problem; now there is a crisis: it is part of a
widespread demoralisation in our society'.(18)
    Between the current uncertainties of both
undergraduate English and the middle years of the
secondary school the Advanced level course appears
to offer comparative security to teachers and
pupils. Although it is under constant discussion and
review, its content and demands represent for many
English teachers the unity remembered by Frank
Whitehead which has disappeared from the rest of the
school.

> In the early sixties the prevailing mood among
> enlightened teachers of English was one of
> hopefulness ... they believed that English
> teaching was a unity, but that the experience
> of literature, broadly conceived, must be a
> central component of that unity - almost, one
> might say, the corner stone upon which the
> arch depended ...; the beginning English teacher
> today moves into a scene that is riven by
> factions, uncertain, confused, lacking a clear
> sense of direction, often dispirited, sometimes
> betraying signs of malaise that comes peril-
> ously close to demoralisation.(19)

Part of the purpose of this book, however, is to
suggest that this security and unity are, especially
for our pupils, more apparent than real.

NOTES

    1.   J.R. Squire and R.K. Applebee, Teaching
English in the United Kingdom (USA National Council
of Teachers of English, 1969) p. 43.
    2.   Edmond Holmes, What Is and What Might
Be (London, Constable, 1911) p. 129.

3.   James Britton, postscript to Robert Druce, The Eye of Innocence (Leicester, Brockhampton Press, 1965).

4.   Herbert Read, Education through Art (Faber and Faber, London, 1943) pp. 68-69.

5.   Lawrence Stenhouse, 'Open-Minded Teaching', New Society, July 24, 1969.

6.   The Humanities Course, Student's Guide, The Bosworth College, Desford, Leicester.

7.   Squire and Applebee, Teaching English in the United Kingdom, p. 870.

8.   E.P. Clark, 'Language and Politics in Education', English in Education, 5, 2, (Summer 1971), p. 102.

9.   Half Our Future (London, HMSO, 1963), p. 153.

10.  H. Rosen, Language Study, the Teacher and the Learner (London, Edward Arnold, 1973), pp. 40f.

11.  Peet and Robinson, The Critical Examination, p. 70.

12.  B. Harries, unpublished M.Ed. thesis, 'The Study of T.S. Eliot in a college of education: problems of analysis and understanding', Leicester University, 1975.

13.  Steiner, Language and Silence, p. 79.

14.  Colin McCabe, 'Complete diversity - or disarray?' The Times Higher Education Supplement, p. 13.

15.  Mulhern, The Moment of Scrutiny, pp. 323-324.

16.  Hollingworth, p. 4.

17.  Terence Hawkes, 'Complete diversity - or disarray?', p. 12.

18.  David Holbrook, English for Meaning (NFER Windsor, 1979), p. 9.

19.  Frank Whitehead, 'Stunting the Growth. The Present State of English Teaching', The Use of English, 28, 1, Autumn, 1976, pp. 11-12.

Chapter Four

EASING THE PACE: SOME SUGGESTIONS

How can teachers ease first year sixth formers'
entry into the activity of observant, personally
involved reading which Advanced level examiners will
reward in their written answers at the end of the
course? Although, as we have noted, examiners are
often inconsistent about their aims in the practical
criticism papers, they all claim to be looking for
evidence of pupils' readiness to relate what they
read to their own experiences and of their ability
to recognise the purpose of writers' choice and
arrangement of language, using the minimum critical
terminology. It might be argued that, in view of all
the uncertainties surrounding the desired balance
which examiners seek between personal response and
technical analysis, they ought to consider introducing some changes into these papers. They might
give helpful information about the historical context of the chosen pieces, and glossaries of unfamiliar words, if they are serious about elim-
inating accidental advantages which pupils bring
to this examination. They might consider setting
passages singly for close attention, instead of
expecting comparisons and evaluations in a short
examination period. Most helpfully, they might
consider setting a wider range of tasks designed to
evaluate the perceived quality of pupils' responses
to literature. Pupils could be asked to prepare
readings of poems and prose passages; or to produce
pieces of creative writing to show their understanding of the selected material. Until dissatisfied Advanced level English teachers succeed in
bringing pressure upon examination boards to review
their practice in the practical criticism papers,
the best they can do is to introduce some of these
activities into their lessons, especially during
the first year. Too many pupils, it appears, are

forced, too soon, across the wide gulf which currently exists between the best examinations in
English at CSE and Ordinary level, and those currently set at Advanced level.

The suggestions which follow are intended to
increase pupils' confidence in the value of their
own responses to imaginative literature and to
sharpen their awareness of the kind of questions
to ask themselves about poems and prose passages.
Although they are broadly grouped into teacher
directed and pupil centred strategies it is hoped
that teachers will take both approaches in the
sixth form - the non interventionist, pupil
initiated, creative approaches which characterise
the most effective English teaching in our junior
and middle schools and the teacher directed, analytical approaches taken in traditional sixth form
courses. In the first group of suggestions, though
they are for mainly teacher directed lessons,
teachers will be asked to elicit their pupils'
experience and knowledge which relates to the
selected material as a preliminary to the initial
readings. In the second, pupil centred, set of
suggestions, they will be asked to give sixth
formers responsibility for preparing public
readings, leading group discussions and producing
pieces of writing based upon the poems and prose
passages.

Because most sixth formers lack some of the
experience and much of the knowledge which makes
adult literature readily accessible, they need
preparation and guidance in order to avoid unnecessary misinterpretations which might undermine
their confidence. On this question, decisions have
to be made both about the amount and nature of
appropriate information and explanation, and about
whether it is the teachers' or pupils' responsibility to provide it. The main point here is that,
before the whole class can reasonably be asked to
respond to, or interpret, a poem or prose passage,
all pupils should have had made available such
information as will enable them to make sense of it.

Throughout the Advanced level course teachers
should always be asking themselves how they can
introduce, through the tasks they set and the
questions they raise, those minimum technical considerations pupils are expected to include in their
written examination answers. It is hoped that pupils
will gradually become aware of their responsibility
to recognise the poet's or novelist's central concern - the subject, or content, that they will

become increasingly observant about whose point
of view or attitude is being given and the author's/
narrator's/speaker's intended audience. Class discussions, preparation of public readings, and personal writing stimulated by selected literature,
should all help pupils to recognise, as well, how
writers shape their material and how they choose and
arrange language to re-create experience.


TEACHER DIRECTED LESSONS


## Introductions: Eliciting pupils' experience and knowledge

Many teachers present poems and prose passages for
analysis, even in the first year of the sixth form,
without introductions. They usually allow time for
silent readings, after the first public reading,
which are followed by questions on the chosen
material. Teachers taking this approach appear
to fear lest introductions diminish the literature's
immediacy of impact and interfere with pupils'
spontaneous and sincere responses. Some, bearing
the Advanced level examination in mind, believe
that the 'deep end' approach is the best preparation
for what is to come. It seems highly likely, though,
that if this approach is taken too early in the
Advanced level course, it will produce a gulf
between the more and less confident members of
the class, the less confident pupils and their
teacher and, most serious, between all the pupils
and the writer, especially the poet. Neglect
of preparation of some kind, by teachers or pupils,
can have the effect of reducing class participation
because of pupils' lack of confidence in their
ability to make sense of what they read.
    If one of our central concerns in the new
sixth form is to avoid these divisions, we must take
great care with our introductions to new material.
It may be necessary sometimes, however undesirable,
to take two periods over a poem or prose passage, in
order to include an appropriate introduction, an
initial reading aloud, full discussion, and at least
one rereading. Two important decisions have to be
made, thus, about how to use the time most effectively before the first reading of unfamiliar
material. Firstly, we have to decide what to focus
upon: either the 'content' or some aspect of it; or

the title and how it anticipates and organises the poem; or historical background and unfamiliar vocabulary; or striking stylistic features. Secondly, we have to decide whether to ask for pupils' contributions or to provide the introduction ourselves.

In the junior and middle school, a familiar approach before reading a poem or prose passage is to invite pupils to contribute factual information, or experiences and opinions which relate closely to the chosen material. Young children are often asked to exchange facts and/or feelings about animals, places, seasons, situations and dilemmas before being invited to recognise similarities and differences between their own and writers' views on a subject. My first proposal is that we should consider how this approach might be adapted to our work with first year sixth formers. Inviting pupils to talk about what they know and feel means that the lesson opens with their contributions, that the experiences they bring to the classroom are treated seriously and that they may be more willing, as a consequence, to offer comments, later, on the material itself. Most importantly, a preliminary exchange can develop pupils' awareness of what they share and how they differ from each other, and when it is related to the chosen text, suggest that there is value in their personal responses to imaginative writers' treatment of experience.

Before reading Lawrence's 'Snake' in the middle school, teachers are likely to explore pupils' knowledge and experience of the physical features of snakes of different kinds in anticipation of the poet's fascination with his snake's compelling beauty and dignity. Before a sixth form reading it might be valuable to explore pupils' feelings about our moral stance on the animal world. The poem recreates an encounter which produces conflicting emotions, a sudden decision and its aftermath of moral distress. To prepare for their personal involvement in the poet's communication of his experience pupils might be asked to reflect for several minutes on what they regard as the rights and wrongs of killing animals. Most groups respond with initial certainties: animals in pain should be destroyed; man should not maim or kill animals for entertainment or the pursuit of profit. Uncertainties enter very soon, of course, about matters of communities' livelihoods and, more controversially, about issues relating to quality of human life. The central point of this initial discussion is to prepare for relating pupils' knowledge and awareness

of uncertainties and moral distress to one of the
main areas of the poem's experience. After expressing their own views, worries, strong feelings, and
hearing those of others in the groups, pupils can be
invited to be observant about what exactly produces
similar confusion in the poet's mind and to consider
how he attempts to resolve it and with what consequences. We have found that pupils who have been
given the  opportunity to think for a brief period
about the question of danger and threats posed by
animal life respond quickly to the apparent serenity
and harmlessness of Lawrence's snake - 'as drinking
cattle do' - in the opening section and recognise
the dilemma which the conflict between two different
sorts of knowledge produces in this poem.

Sometimes we may seek only factual information
from our pupils - about animals, places, seasons,
historical events - to encourage class participation
and to introduce a sense of familiarity with the
chosen writer. Sixth formers, I am suggesting, can
benefit as much as younger pupils from being invited
to reflect initially upon their own experience of
some aspect of what the writer is re-creating. This
can draw them into consideration of whose voice he
is speaking with, his attitude towards his
'subject', the  ways in which he arranges language
to communicate what centrally concerns him. Pupils'
responses to the experience which the chosen writer
explores can introduce the process of engagement
which is extended and refined during their close
reading of the material.

## Introductions: Titles

These can sometimes determine our choice of introduction to new material. Attention to the words in
a title can prepare pupils for a writer's attitude
towards his 'subject matter', can introduce the
contradictions, or tensions, or specially powerful
feelings in the poem. Consider, for example, Andrew
Marvell's 'To his Coy Mistress'. In view of the
poem's content, organisation, attitudes, features of
style (changes of tense, striking imagery) time is
well spent on exploring what pupils understand by
both 'coy' and 'mistress', and in inviting suggestions about the sorts of approaches and arguments
which they might expect her admirer to put to the
lady. Someone might be asked to say, or to do something coyly, and pupils' views invited about the
hints it gives about the performer's personality.
Initial discussion might alternatively be limited to

the changing meanings of these words and to anticipating unfamiliar vocabulary in the poem. If time
allows, however, we have found it helpful to penetrate beyond that into pupils' understanding of coy-
ness and some of its consequences for sexual relationships. Few fail to anticipate something of the
poet's exasperated sexual urgency, their sense of
which is likely to deepen when they experience his
powerful awareness and re-creation of the passing of
time.

A similar approach can helpfully introduce 'The
Love Song of J. Alfred Prufrock', that is, it can
prepare pupils for the poem's central tensions which
are anticipated by the title. Initial reflection
about 'love songs' quickly produces associations of
youth, desire, confidence, strong emotions, communication between singer and audience. 'J. Alfred
Prufrock', when given equally close attention,
produces associations of modern business life, board
room doors, letter headings, formality and imperson-
ality. What kind of love song might he be expected
to sing? And to whom? Consideration of these contradictions within this title can prepare for the pupils'
entry, however initially confused, into part of the
emotional territory of the poem and can be employed
to organise class discussion around the poet's
re-creation of the public and private worlds of
Prufrock. Even after a first reading, pupils who
have been invited to anticipate the central concerns
of the chosen material begin to find their bearings
and have enough confidence to contribute their early
observations on aspects which they recognise.

One last example of when it might be valuable
to spend the opening minutes of a lesson on a poem's
title is 'Anthem for Doomed Youth'. In our experience few pupils are confident about what an anthem
is and where and why it is sung. Since much of the
force of Owen's uncertainty about the appropriate
way to mourn those destroyed in battle comes from
the contrast between the ritual of church burial and
the noise of gunfire, this is either diminished or
lost entirely if pupils fail to recognise the context of his religious imagery. Teachers have to
decide, according to their knowledge of a group,
how valuable it might be to explore its appreciation
of 'anthem' and 'doomed'. It is highly likely that,
with promptings through references to familiar
public mournings and national events, their understanding will easily be elicited; if this fails,
then teachers need to give explanations and examples.
The main point here is that, without the confidence

which comes from having a sense of the emotional,
moral or physical territory they are about to enter,
many pupils will be unwilling to express their
personal responses to new writing. To have discovered
themselves or to have been given access to knowledge and understanding of crucial meanings, con-
cepts, experiences or references, <u>before</u> the initial
reading, is immensely helpful to many pupils. It has
taken them part of the way into the poems, introducing possibilities for discussion of personal
sympathy, or hostility  to what they find. Titles,
in our experience, are infrequently mentioned in
practical criticism lessons. We have observed
lessons - on 'Byzantium', 'Bavarian Gentians',
'Musée des Beaux Arts' - in which no attempt has
been made to discover what, if anything, these mean
to pupils and to indicate how they introduce the
central concerns of the poems.

## Organisation
Consideration of titles and ways in which they
frequently anticipate the poems' experiences leads
directly to a possible extension of this preparation
which some groups might find helpful. Before the
first reading the teacher might make a brief statement about the organisation of the poem or prose
passage. Many teachers, I have already noted, are
strongly opposed to this because it goes too far,
in their view, towards imposing their own readings
and leaves too little space for pupils' own discoveries. Like the other suggestions in this chapter it
is not intended to be employed with every poem and
prose passage; it is sometimes a valuable approach
to take early in the sixth form with a group which
lacks confidence about how to talk about new
material. Once the shape of the poem or prose
passage has been described, its importance can be
reinforced if class discussion is organised around
it. So much remains still to be discovered, noted
and shared that, once again, to prepare an entry
into the material can raise pupils' confidence and
help them collect their thoughts. Returning firstly
to Marvell's poem. If pupils are told that, in the
first part the poet considers what he might do if
all the time and space in the world were available,
in the second reminds his mistress that it is not,
and finally, makes his proposal, they can reasonably
be asked to be observant about some of the ways in
which he communicates his thoughts and feelings at
each of these stages of his address. Whether pupils

are asked to prepare readings which convey Marvell's
attitude towards his mistress - intended to stimulate class discussion about regret, irony, exaspera-
tion, urgency - or whether the teacher directs their
attention, didactically, to tenses and conceits, the
point is that, having been given the poem's plan,
pupils can focus upon other features of Marvell's
language.

This approach can be employed, of course, with
all new extracts, and is helpful in introducing and
developing the notion of writers' organisation of
their material. The feature of shape, or organisation, is best understood when class discussion is
deliberately structured afterwards to strengthen
pupils' awareness of how it re-creates the central
experience and they are encouraged to focus upon
how each section relates to the next. Before the
first reading, for example, of 'Ode on Melancholy', pupils can be told that at the beginning
the poet is looking at and addressing the work
of art as a whole; he then looks more closely
at the scenes depicted on it, then re-creates imag-
ined scenes suggested by its decorations and finally
stands back, as it were, and contemplates the whole
again. Most teachers will want to spend most of
their pupils' time on questions of poet and audience/
reader and, even more importantly, on how the
richness of Keats' figurative language realises his
feelings about this work of art. We have found,
though, that many pupils appreciate being given help
both with unfamiliar vocabulary and with the way
this poem develops before being asked to give it
close attention. One of our central concerns in this
work is to confer value upon what pupils understand
and feel about new literature which they meet. In
every poem and prose passage of value there will be
much to comment upon and to explore. Some considerations can be usefully treated before the material is
read as a way of giving pointers and guidelines
towards what to expect, thus leaving pupils free to
move into other areas of interest. In Ted Hughes'
'November', for example, there is much to be noticed
and discussed about the poet's arresting impressions
and the ways in which they convey the effect of the
harsh landscape upon him. A brief introduction
which outlines the shape of this poem opens the way
for close concentration about its specially interesting stylistic features. Firstly, Hughes describes
himself in the sodden landscape; secondly, he
describes his reactions to the sleeping tramp;

thirdly, the weather worsens; fourthly, he rushes
into what appear to be the protective woods.

Before asking pupils to look closely at other
features of the prose passages chosen for discussion
later in this book, teachers might choose to map
their organisation as a way of giving new readers
their initial bearings. Written from one viewpoint
the early passages about childhood are fairly
straightforward. Some pupils, nevertheless, might
be helped by being told, before closer consideration
of the extract from Huckleberry Finn, that Mark
Twain's speaker tells the reader firstly about
his life in general and then about one evening
of his life. Informed about the main shift of
interest in the passage, pupils can then be asked to
look for the factual information which each section
contains and later at the speaker's attitudes towards the Widow and her sister. Before exploring
the extract from A High Wind in Jamaica pupils
can be told that the narrator's description begins
inside, and then moves outside the house. Confident
about location, they can look for information about
the narrator and the effects of the storm upon her.
This kind of help is likely to be most appreciated
when given, either as preliminary information or as
questions to be considered, before pupils are asked
to explore passages containing a variety of viewpoints. Many pupils welcome, in the early stages of
this work, being given guidance of this kind before
approaching passages as complex as George Eliot's
account of Dorothea's marriage prospects. If they
have been prepared to meet the cautious suitor,
rural opinion and Dorothea's view of herself within
George Eliot's presentation of the question, they
are better prepared to give focused attention to the
ways in which these differ and how the author handles
them. It is one way of helping new readers to
avoid feeling overwhelmed by the variety of impressions created by an unfamiliar piece of writing.

Outline maps of poems and prose passages, or a
number of points to consider when preparing oral or
written comments - movements from one area to
another; from one time to another; from reasons to
consequences; from major to minor considerations;
from one viewpoint to another - introduce sixth
form readers to notions of organisation and shape.
On approaching prose passages, especially, teachers'
introductions to the relationship between narrator
and material can sharpen pupils' awareness of
changing viewpoints. If pupils gradually grow
accustomed to noticing the titles of poems and

where poets stand in relation to their subject
matter and audience; if they are regularly reminded
about changes in place, time and viewpoint in
poetry and prose, they may gain confidence about
their own observations upon what they read. We hope
that they will soon begin to ask themselves these
questions about literature which they encounter for
the first time and are required to explore in an
appreciative way.


## Readability

In the junior and middle school many English
teachers anticipate the confusion likely to be produced in pupils by unfamiliar vocabulary in new
material. Evidence suggests that, of all subject
teachers, they consider the readability of literature and adopt helpful strategies to avoid bewilder-
ment.(1) They realise that pupils who do not know
what hawks do when they roost, or what is meant by
'batman' or 'his father's school' (in The Rocking
Horse Winner) cannot reasonably be asked probing
questions about more important features of the
poem or short story.
 This kind of anticipation is often curiously
neglected once pupils are in the sixth form. Here,
however, loss of confidence is likely to be most
destructive and now is when the teacher needs to be
especially sensitive to the importance of all his
pupils beginning their reading of unfamiliar literature at the same point. Their difficulties will be
of different kinds. In lessons on 'Snake' we have
met pupils in the lower sixth who did not know that
Etna is a volcano (with strange consequences for the
line where it appears) and were unfamiliar with the
story of the albatross. Whilst these are worth
anticipating and explaining, the verb 'expiate' can
be left until the discussion which will follow about
Lawrence's sense of self disgust and lost opportunity. Unfamiliar vocabulary in current use is often
best grappled with during the discussion which takes
place after public and private readings, or made
part of directed individual or group preparation of
readings and opening short talks. Historical,
literary, technical and personal allusions, however,
unless - as in T.S. Eliot's poetry, for example -
they are inseparable from the text - need to be
explained or explored beforehand for the passage to
make some sort of impact. Most pupils we have met
have not, as I have noted, encountered 'anthem' and
'passing bells' and 'orisons' before reading Owen's

poem, have not known what Bavarian gentians are in
Lawrence's poem and are thus seriously hampered in
their efforts to respond to the experience of the
poems. Teachers face several initial decisions. They
have to distinguish between the kind of difficulties the literature is likely to present; decide
when to handle them; in how much detail; and who is
best placed to provide the explanations. Sometimes
poems are full of classical references which most
pupils are unlikely to have met previously - the
classical allusions in Keats' odes (Lethe, psyche in
'Melancholy'; Tempe, Arcady in 'Ode on a Grecian
Urn'). Sometimes there will be references to the
natural world, like Etna, or wolfsbane or globed
peonies. Sometimes apparently familiar words, like
'nature' or 'vegetable' or 'polite', will have
changed their meaning; sometimes familiar words will
be used in an unfamiliar way - the 'allotment' of
death; the 'let' of a ditch. Several strategies are
available of course - giving a selection of explanations, enquiring from pupils about their available
specialist information, asking individuals, pairs or
groups, to research words and terms in readiness for
introducing a public reading of a poem or passage.
Any of these is preferable to giving out copies,
reading, or having the poem read, and asking a series
of questions which are answered by a dwindling
number of the confident minority, or in which the
level of questioning alternates capriciously between demands for explanations of 'difficult' words
(what does psyche mean?) and personal responses
(what do you think the poet wants us to feel...?)

## Background
Related closely to the problem of handling unfamiliar vocabulary and explanation of allusions is the
question of 'background', of period or writers'
personal lives. Usually it is interesting and helpful for pupils to be told a little, by the teacher
or fellow pupils, about special features of the
period, a writer's life, his central concerns,
before more specific questions are explored. Too
much information, however, especially if the context
is too broad, can be bewildering and unhelpful.
Lessons which begin with mini-lectures on metaphysical poetry, the heroic couplet, the romantic
period, Yeats' personal life and choice of symbols,
leave too little time for reading and discussion.
Even when pupils are invited to undertake some
introductory explanations their value as 'pupil

participation' can be diminished if they have not received guidance about what precisely to focus upon, and consequently off load a jumble of material which bears little relation to the chosen points. Too little 'background' is probably to be preferred to too much, if it takes the form of inappropriately long general talks, bulky handouts, or dictated notes which erode the time available for observant, questioning close reading.

We shall be considering 'A Valediction: forbidding mourning' in detail in the next section. I introduce it here because the verse about the spheres is a good example of when background information is essential if pupils are not to be justifiably confused at this stage of the poem. There is too much of greater importance – questions of speaker and audience, the organisation of Donne's argument, the contrasts between spiritual and physical love, the function of the figurative language – to invite pupils to notice, understand and exchange views about, to allow their ignorance of seventeenth century perspectives on cosmology and earthquakes to put obstacles in their way. Very brief explanatory notes can be given with copies of the poem along with some questions to be thought about, ahead of the lesson. If it is to be read for the first time in class the teacher can (after, it is recommended, a few moments have been spent on 'valediction' and 'mourning') supply the necessary information. Or, if pupils are going to analyse a number of Donne's poems, they can be asked to follow up specific scientific questions and be ready to give explanations appropriate to each poem's references.

My purpose in concentrating upon introductions to poems and prose has been to suggest ways of treating unfamiliar literature in class which will give all our pupils confidence in their ability to read and respond to it. Broadly speaking, there are two ways to treat the 'content', the titles, the organisation, the allusions and unfamiliar vocabulary – telling and asking. All pupils will bring knowledge and experience to our lessons which can be probed, articulated and closely related to the concerns of imaginative writers. How can this be elicited and shared, and then related to the selected material, and refined and extended through involvement in writer's choice and arrangement of language? How much, additionally, is it essential for all pupils to be told before they can be reasonably asked to engage with the material? If you do

not know what Lethe is, it is not within your power
to offer your explanation of the reason for Keats'
repeated negatives with which 'Ode on Melancholy'
opens. If you do not know what a gentian looks like,
or what a hawk is doing when it is roosting, you are
severely hampered in your efforts to appreciate the
flower's and bird's special significance for
Lawrence and Hughes.

## PUPILS' ACTIVITIES

To develop confidence in their ability to make sense
of what they read, and in the value of their own
responses, pupils need to be given frequent opportunities to interpret literature for themselves. We
should try to find ways, in the sixth form, not only
of making unfamiliar literature accessible to pupils
but of making pupils responsible for communicating
their responses to others. Ideally, time should be
found both for lessons which derive from teachers'
readings of literature and for sessions in which
pupils lead discussions, give public readings, and
take part in oral and written activities stimulated
by the poetry, prose passages and drama. In pupil
centred activities it might be possible to achieve
a fusion of close, observant, questioning reading,
and whatever we understand by the personal, individual response which literature invites.

### Reading Aloud

Most especially as questions of the identities and
attitudes of speakers and audiences are concerned,
pupils can be asked to prepare public readings for
the enjoyment and critical attention of the rest of
the class. As well as hearing well prepared readings
by their teachers and professional actors, pupils
should be invited to approve and criticise readings
prepared by individuals, pairs and groups. It is
helpful, as a preparation for regular public readings by pupils, to begin this work upon novels,
short stories and plays which the groups already
know or are reading together as their set texts. In
the first term of many sixth forms most pupils are
meeting as a group for the first time and have come
from a wide range of approaches to English. Taking
extracts from prose and drama, therefore, which
everyone knows or is getting to know has several
advantages: it provides a common experience about

which everyone has some prior knowledge; the material will be familiar, which should mean that everyone approaches the task with some confidence and can have a point of view about the readers' effectiveness; the task links what are often seen by pupils as separate activities, the unseen and the set text, and introduces the notions of the author's/speaker's personality, central concern, audience, tone of voice, choice and arrangement of language.

Most sixth formers will have taken part in dramatised readings of novels and short stories, as readers and listeners, earlier in the school. They are experienced, therefore, in reading aloud and hearing texts in which feelings about places, events and people have been communicated in a variety of ways. Extracts from familiar writers such as Stan Barstow, Alan Sillitoe, William Golding and D.H. Lawrence might make the best starting points for public readings and critical listening. Additionally, extracts might be taken from the prose works being studied on the Advanced level syllabus. Individuals, pairs or small groups can be asked to prepare readings of descriptive passages, narrative, dialogue and complete episodes for the rest of the class to enjoy and to raise questions about chosen interpretations. Pupils tend to enjoy literature more when they recognise voices behind the printed word, which might explain why less capable readers tend to prefer narrative poetry to highly imagistic poetry, or drama to non fiction prose. Pupils, especially in the sixth form, sometimes need to be reminded that all literature is essentially dramatic in nature, whether the literature is a soliloquy, a monologue or a dialogue. If they can be regularly involved in activities which require them to respond to a speaker - speaking for him and, in other, related activities, responding to him, or creating a scene 'off stage' with him - they are being asked to be observant about the language which he is employing.

Most pupils are likely to be willing to take part in preparation of public performances of dialogue taken from twentieth century prose. Those who are reluctant to read aloud can become involved in searching the selected texts for information which serves as evidence for characters' motivation and bears upon how they will speak in dramatic context. Gradually they should be getting used to explaining decisions about interpretation by reference to the situations, the subject matter, the movement

of the scene and, most importantly, the selection
and arrangement of the author's language.

A second stage on the way to pupils' preparation of public readings of poems might be for them
to explore speeches and scenes from Shakespeare.
Again, the best approach might be through familiar
texts or through those being studied in other parts
of the course. Begin, perhaps, with well known,
short exchanges such as those between Macbeth and
Lady Macbeth before and after Duncan's murder.
Drawing upon the methods demonstrated in the recent
Channel Four series on Acting Shakespeare, teachers
might choose a selection of short scenes for pupils
to experiment with, either to write up reports on
their decisions or to 'produce' for the rest of the
class. Victoria O'Brien's helpful book, <u>Playing
Shakespeare</u>, provides teachers with a wide variety
of strategies designed to encourage pupils to search
the texts for their own interpretations. In the
section for older pupils engaged in academic study
of the plays she suggests 'charting the emotional
pattern in big scenes'. Describing approaches for
directed watchfulness over complete plays, she re-
commends that pupils occasionally be asked to
experiment with interpreting some of the major
speeches. If they know the plays and can be asked
to take careful account of the precise occasion on
which a character speaks in this way, pupils might
be asked to prepare, say, Anthony's prophecy over
Caesar's body, or Macbeth's uncertainties about
Duncan's murder. Divide the class into pairs or
small groups, with the instruction to work out how
they believe a particular speech should be spoken:
consider who is speaking, where, when, to whom,
about what, in what mood, with what intention.
Attention must be given to variations in volume,
pace, pauses, intonation, emphasis, and attention
must be given to these matters by the listeners
during the delivery of these speeches. If everyone
has copies of the speeches and all are familiar
with what have been allocated, then they are both
performers and audiences in these sessions and all
can participate at some stage of the exercise. If
pupils can be given plentiful experience in preparing prose passages and fairly difficult encount-
ers and speeches in plays, they will be appropriate-
ly introduced to the central points for consideration when they prepare to read poems aloud.
Teachers', and professional, readings are vital to
encourage effective public reading. But of equal
importance is the discussion which takes place

amongst pupils about the age, sex, status of characters and their attitudes towards their audiences.
Whilst this activity needs to be given direction by
the questions raised by the teacher for consideration by readers and their listeners, time should be
generous for preparation of at least one reading
from each group followed by listeners' assessment of
their effectiveness. After varied work on speeches
from plays from different periods, pupils might
begin reading poetry by way of Shakespeare's sonnets,
metaphysical poetry, Browning's and T.S. Eliot's
dramatic monologues. Presentations can be given
mainly in class, that is, in the Advanced level
group, bearing in mind the demands of the practical
criticism paper. They can be prepared with tape
recorders, perhaps with the addition of short
explanatory introductions; they can be presented on
more public occasions, in societies or school
functions or, if the school is organised in this
way, prepared for competitions adjudicated by
sensitive professionals who appreciate the attempt
to make links between examination demands and dramatic performances. The important point is that
pupils have been given responsibility for interpretations, for expressing personal response to the
whole poem or passage, which represent their understanding of matters such as speaker and audience,
attitude, organisation and stylistic features.
Unless these points have been fully considered, the
reading, whilst it might be effective in the hands
of a 'good' reader, will not stand up to subsequent
enquiry and discussion.
    Preparing poems and prose passages for reading
aloud needs to be a central activity throughout the
whole course. As pupils gain confidence and experience they can be asked to do this after fairly
short periods of preparation and can be given responsibility for reading poems which are unfamiliar
to the rest of the group. By the second year pupils
should be familiar with the central questions about
subject matter, speaker and audience, organisation,
recurrent imagery, arresting stylistic features. By
then they can be given assignments which involve
them in preparing to give explanatory comments,
noting unusual effects and to answer questions asked
by the rest of the class.


Notes; drafts; essays
Preparation for reading aloud and for critical
listening involves pupils in writing about

literature. It involves them in committing themselves, initially in note form, to what they make
of the text, to what a passage, a speech, a dialogue,
a scene, a poem, is about - its 'theme', 'content'
or 'subject matter', to take terms from the examination papers. Notes may be written by pupils individually, or may be prepared by groups during planning
for public performances. Notes help to direct the
readers on matters of writers' or speakers' attitudes. Like directors' notes on play scripts for
rehearsals, they provide pupils with material with
which to defend and explain their decisions about
intentions and motivations discovered in the texts.

If pupils are encouraged to take account of
features which are becoming familiar during teacher
directed lessons, note taking of this kind can be
used as starting points for pieces of continuous
writing about poems and prose passages. These can be
handed in periodically for teachers to assess the
quality of pupils' observations and written expression. Notes, therefore, can lead to drafting and
redrafting. What begins as a set of scribbled comments can be developed into an account of what the
reader judges to be the meaning of a passage, an
account which attempts to integrate what a writer
is saying and how he says it.

It might be helpful to remind ourselves, at
this point, that experienced teachers of literature
at Advanced level appear to be concerned about two
main problems: how to handle subjectivity and
objectivity; and how to encourage pupils to handle
the inseparability of content and form. Pat D'Arcy
writes about the first of these:

> How far our interpretation of a literary text
> tallies exactly with the meaning the writer
> intended, can, in the long run, only be a sub-
> jective assessment. Teachers differ as widely
> in their initial responses to an unfamiliar
> text as their students do. Our argument would
> be that the impossibility of absolutely 'right'
> or 'wrong' responses needs to be recognition
> that the joint exploration of a text through
> discussion and through writing about it, can
> lead to a sharing of perceptions which con-
> verge more closely in their grasp of meaning.
> Otherwise there would be little point in
> studying novels, plays and poems together.(2)

Richard Gill, reviewing a number of related problems
of which he is aware when teaching poetry,

especially, directs his readers' attention to the matter of relationship of content and form. Pupils and students, he argues, find it difficult to talk, and it follows, to write, about poetry 'in such a way as to suggest that the content is present in and through the form, yet, at the same time, make clear that form and content are not two things, but terms which describe one reality - the words?' Acknowledging that there is no easy answer to this problem, he says that what he tries to do is 'to encourage the students to write about how they feel the meaning is enacted in the words of the poem'.(3)

Teacher directed lessons can try to take account of both these difficulties. I have already suggested some ways in which introductions and directed discussions about poetry and prose might reconcile pupils' knowledge and experience with strong personal readings which determine teachers' decisions about the emphasis in their lessons. Shared discussions amongst pupils provide further opportunities for approaching these problems. And for these to take off they often need, in the early stages, to grow out of written material, both notes and extended commentaries.

After giving out copies of a poem, ask pupils - on their own or in pairs - to write down what they make of it. Ask them, perhaps in a work sheet, to reflect upon and record what it is about, how it is organised and how the poet's choice and arrangement of language supports their views. These jottings can be handled in various ways. They can be handed in for the teacher to note the main similarities and differences and to present these to the group at the next meeting. They can be exchanged amongst the group for pupils' immediate recognition of likely diversity, and for further note taking on points of agreement and disagreement. Pupils might read out their notes, when developed for confident presentation, for the others to record points with which to introduce general discussion. It is hoped that this give and take between individual readings and shared exploration will raise pupils' awareness of the balance we are seeking between subjectivity and objectivity throughout the course.

Like Richard Gill, Pat D'Arcy expresses her concern also about pupils' difficulties with the relationship between meaning and style, or content and form. In common with other commentators on the Advanced level examination both teachers are keenly aware of the differences between how we read and how the examiners appear to be asking pupils to write on the 'unseen' papers. Pat D'Arcy concludes, after considering a group of teachers' responses to a speech from Othello and an unseen poem:

> The majority of teachers wrote about 'meaning', which is the sum of what is being said, how it is said, by whom, to whom, where, what was said before, and a myriad of other considerations. It seems to me that the use of the word 'style' is a hindrance: we should concentrate on the process by which meaning is carried by utterance and the process by which it is retrieved.(4)

We can try to help our pupils in this matter of content and form both by our conduct of class discussion and by how we encourage them to write about literature. We need to introduce, anticipate and remind pupils about, specific points such as titles, writers' and speakers' attitudes towards their subject matter, organisation and 'effective irregularities' of language. And we need to encourage expression of their awareness of these points when they make their first jottings. Later they can be asked to recast these observations into sharper and more discriminating versions of their first readings. When these have been shared, with fellow pupils or the teacher, and checked for omissions, repetitions and poor expression, the final versions might be prepared, either for the Advanced level folder, or to serve as models upon which to base later work of this kind.

Examiners reported upon two recurrent weaknesses in Advanced level scripts, incoherence and vagueness. If pupils are encouraged to work from notes, made either for class readings and performances, or for drafts of essays to be exchanged with others in their group, they may gradually gain confidence about referring directly to the text to support the meanings which they find there. The following comments in a successful Advanced level pupil's work illustrate the sort of precision we hope to encourage. Writing about 'Dictionary' after considering 'Blue Umbrellas' she observes:

> 'Dictionary' is organised into an orderly structure with nine verses of a regular three lines. This orderliness reflects the structure of the book it is describing in which everything is set out neatly and uniformly. The poem describes the importance of the book, so familiar to all of us today, and yet totally

inadequate to <u>tell</u> us anything because it
reduces everything to an ordinary, conventional
plane ... The book is next personified as if
indeed it has become a human god. Other books
are '<u>feeling</u>' humbled: it swallowed them all
before they existed'. They can say nothing that
has not been stated before and has therefore
been categorised and listed into position, 'its
belly' has digested inspirational thoughts and
come out with orderly rows of words lacking any
'life'.(5)

## Personal Writing

An additional pupil centred activity, which demands
understanding of, and their personal response to,
the selected material, is their creative writing
which it is hoped that close reading has stimulated.
In many continuously assessed CSE courses pupils are
invited to make a 'personal' or 'creative' response
to literature as expression of their involvement in
the experience of a poem, a play, or prose extract.
We have been persistently impressed by the quality
of many pupils' stories or dialogues written after
studying Stan Barstow's 'The Fury', which reveal
their sensitivity to the precise nature of the
story's central conflict, as well as by poems stimulated by D.H. Lawrence and Ted Hughes, which show
pupils' understanding of how these poets have
re-created their unique physical surroundings. We
suggest that this activity should be extended
into the sixth form, not only because many pupils
enjoy it and miss it on their Advanced level course.
We think that what is involved in creating scenes,
dialogues, narratives and descriptions which develop
some aspects of the material they have studied can
achieve that fusion of personal response and observant reading which we are seeking in practical
criticism. In order to compose a reply to a
Shakespeare sonnet, or a Donne love poem; to create
a conversation between the speaker in a poem or
prose passage and the implied audience; to develop
an incident in a story or novel successfully, pupils
need to have engaged observantly or personally with
the original material. It is likely that, by the
time they have reached the sixth form, especially
the second year, many pupils will choose not to
give this kind of evidence of their understanding
of literature. Their creative response will be their
engagement with the experience in the poem and prose
passage, their attempts to grapple with everything

it involves. If teachers never invite this response to literature, though, they may be closing off valuable opportunities for some pupils to respond personally to what they read.

NOTES

1. Russell Call and Neal Wiggin (1974) reported by Colin Harrison, Readability in the Classroom (Cambridge University Press, 1980) p. 125.
2. Pat D'Arcy, 'In Search of Style', pp. 13-14.
3. Richard Gill, The New Leicestershire Journal (Issue No. 7, 1983) p. 9.
4. Pat D'Arcy, 'In Search of Style', p. 31.
5. Jayne McNicol, 'Blue Umbrellas' and 'Dictionary' a critical commentary. Guthlaxton School, Leicester.

Chapter Five

APPROACHES TO POEMS: LESSON MATERIAL

Chapter four described two main ways in which
teachers might increase pupils' confidence in their
abilities to make sense of what they read. Its
suggested approaches were presented as teacher
directed and pupil initiated lessons in order to
illustrate and reinforce the view that pupils are
likely to benefit from both experiences. They need
sympathetic guidance on entry into complex, unfamiliar literature and opportunities to explore,
discuss, question and respond on their own and
amongst themselves. Our hope is that they will
gradually ask for themselves the questions raised by
teachers about how writers re-create experience, will
gradually begin to make use of teacher directed lessons to inform and sharpen their own observations.
        What follows is a set of suggestions for
lessons on poems frequently introduced at sixth
form level. These include all the strategies which
were considered in the previous chapter: introductions which draw upon pupils' associations and
expectations; introductions which focus upon titles,
explain unfamiliar allusions and vocabulary and
anticipate organisation and 'features of style'. The
main part of each piece of lesson material consists
of groups of questions which generally follow the
traditional lines of teacher directed close analysis
of poetry.
        This, as the previous chapter emphasised, is
not the only way to approach practical criticism.
Other approaches are well worth considering, even
though they are often much harder work for teachers,
take far more time than conventional lessons and
often produce confusion and frustration. If we are
serious, however, about conferring value upon what
pupils and students make of what they read, we must
show this by giving them frequent opportunities to

explore and discuss on their own. As Peter Clough
reminds us, pupils are not required in teacher
directed lessons to 'pose searching questions which
call for reflection; these questions are part of the
way in which the teacher can direct the enquiry to
her idea of its ends'. Acknowledging that, especially in preparation for examination work, teachers
must intervene, must discriminate between interpretations, Clough insists upon the value of pair and
small group discussion of literature; 'asking
children to spot the areas of their difficulty is
asking them to share in the location of problems'.(1)
The final section of each piece of lesson material
suggests ways in which pupils might work on their
own on the chosen pieces.

It is not intended that these four poems
should be treated in class in the sequence in which
they appear in this section. Although 'Snake' and
'November' might be considered consecutively, it is
likely that most teachers would prefer to read
several of Lawrence's poems and, later, several by
Ted Hughes, with their pupils. Each poem that
follows faces teachers and pupils with different
sorts of difficulties. My intention is to try to
identify these and to suggest ways of overcoming
them.

I

SNAKE    (2)

A snake came to my water-trough
On a hot, hot day, and I in pyjamas for the heat,
To drink there.

In the deep, strange-scented shade of the great dark carob-tree
I came down the steps with my pitcher
And must wait, must stand and wait, for there he was at the trough
        before me.

He reached down from a fissure in the earth-wall in the gloom
And trailed his yellow-brown slackness soft-bellied down, over the
        edge of the stone trough
And rested his throat upon the stone bottom,
And where the water had dripped from the tap, in a small clearness,
He sipped with his straight mouth,
Softly drank through his straight gums, into his slack long body,
Silently.

Someone was before me at my water-trough,
And I, like a second comer, waiting.

He lifted his head from his drinking, as cattle do,
And looked at me vaguely, as drinking cattle do,
And flickered his two-forked tongue from his lips, and mused a moment,
And stooped and drank a little more,
Being earth-brown, earth-golden from the burning bowels of the
        earth
On the day of Sicilian July, with Etna smoking.

The voice of my education said to me
He must be killed,
For in Sicily the black, black snakes are innocent, the gold are venomous.

And voices in me said, If you were a man
You would take a stick and break him now, and finish him off.

But must I confess how I liked him,
How glad I was he had come like a guest in quiet, to drink at my water-
        trough
And depart peaceful, pacified, and thankless,
Into the burning bowels of this earth?

Was it cowardice, that I dared not kill him?
Was it perversity, that I longed to talk to him?
Was it humility, to feel so honoured?
I felt so honoured.


And yet these voices:
*If you were not afraid, you would kill him!*


And truly I was afraid, I was most afraid,
But even so, honoured still more
That he should seek my hospitality
From out the dark door of the secret earth.


He drank enough
And lifted his head, dreamily, as one who has drunken,
And flickered his tongue like a forked night on the air, so black,
Seeming to lick his lips,
And looked around like a god, unseeing, into the air,
And slowly turned his head,
And slowly, very slowly, as if thrice adream,
Proceeded to draw his slow length curving round
And climb again the broken bank of my wall-face.


And as he put his head into that dreadful hole,
And as he slowly drew up, snake-easing his shoulders, and entered
    farther,
A sort of horror, a sort of protest against his withdrawing into that
    horrid black hole,
Deliberately going into the blackness, and slowly drawing himself
    after,
Overcame me now his back was turned.


I looked round, I put down my pitcher,
I picked up a clumsy log
And threw it at the water-trough with a clatter.


I think I did not hit him,
But suddenly that part of him that was left behind convulsed in
    undignified haste,
Writhed like lightning, and was gone
Into the black hole, the earth-lipped fissure in the wall-front,
At which, in the intense still noon, I stared with fascination.


And immediately I regretted it.
I thought how paltry, how vulgar, what a mean act!

I despised myself and the voices of my accursed human education.


And I thought of the albatross,
And I wished he would come back, my snake.


For he seemed to me again like a king,
Like a king in exile, uncrowned in the underworld,
Now due to be crowned again.


And so, I missed my chance with one of the lords
Of life.
And I have something to expiate;
A pettiness.

                                        D.H.  LAWRENCE

I have chosen to consider this poem first because of its likely familiarity. If sixth formers are asked to give close attention to a piece of writing they have already met, they may be prepared to contribute more confidently to class discussion than if faced initially with something unfamiliar. I have chosen it, therefore, for its likely access- ibility. Lawrence's 'subject', his encounter with a venomous snake, tends to provoke powerful associa- tions. The poet addresses the reader directly about his experience. The vocabulary is mainly understood by most sixth formers, and the poet's two most striking 'stylistic features' - personification and repetition - have probably been introduced before and, if not, are easily recognised and related by pupils to the experiences in the poem.

If time can be given on entry into this poem to pupils' reflections upon snakes' likely mystery, fascination and repulsiveness and, during later discussion of the poem, their contributions can be related to the impact this particular snake makes upon the poet, pupils may be helped to recognise Lawrence's reasons for personifying his snake and for writing in ways which draw out each moment of the tense atmosphere which his anxieties create between them. What follows is an account of how some of the approaches introduced in the last chapter might be taken to this poem to encourage pupils' personal response and their recognition of how language re-creates the complexity of the exper- ience. They are all 'teacher directed', that is, they derive from the teacher's reading of this poem, his mapping out for himself the areas for close attention and making decisions about questions of meaning and style which need exploration.


INTRODUCTION

The simplest, and probably the most effective, introduction to this poem is one which focuses upon its title, which immediately provokes uncomfortable associations for most readers. We have found it valuable, even at sixth form level, to spend a few moments upon pupils' reponses to 'snake' and to give them time to share any personal associations, exper- iences and fears. If questions are carefully phrased, pupils' responses can be related later to Lawrence's conflict and the way he resolves it. In every group there will be some expressions of fear and revulsion, even though it is unlikely that anyone will have

been seriously threatened by a snake. If pupils
reflect upon the sources of their anxieties and
disgust, their responses might anticipate Lawrence's
deep confusion about which kind of knowledge he
should trust during his encounter. Uncertainty
frequently emerges in class about exactly how ugly
snakes really are, how slimy (a favourite word) and
how dangerous. Some pupils talk about snakes' beauty,
of colouring, patterning or movement, observed
directly or in television nature programmes. An
opportunity to exchange their responses to different
snakes, to be reminded of the coexistence of conflicting perceptions of snakes, between their own
and famous naturalists' and, perhaps, within themselves, might help pupils to appreciate the conflicting elements in Lawrence's experience.

There are, of course, other areas of pupils'
personal experiences which might be valuably explored before the first public reading of this poem.
As I suggested in the last chapter, pupils' attitudes towards killing animals are likely to reveal
some of our deep, shared uncertainties on this issue
and, if publicly expressed, can anticipate
Lawrence's confusion about how he ought to react to
a venomous snake about which he experiences powerfully warm emotions. Replies to teachers' questions
which are intended to relate to the poet's central
uncertainty about whether a rare, but dangerous,
creature should be killed can lead to the heart of
this poem. They prepare for discussion about the
precise nature of Lawrence's fear - 'If you were not
afraid, you would kill him! And truly I was afraid,
I was most afraid' and, additionally, for recognition of why here, and at other parts of the poem,
he uses repetition for a special kind of emphasis.
If, during the opening discussion, some consideration can be given to our relationships with rare,
though dangerous, animals, a way may have been
opened for appreciation of Lawrence's transformation
of his snake into 'god', 'king' and 'lord' in the
last part of the poem.

Two other possible entries might be made into
this poem, especially if creative writing is to be
invited later as a way of assessing pupils' involvement with Lawrence's experience. Teachers might
decide to focus initial discussion on the issues
underlying one of his statements, made either before
or after his decision about how to act, as starting
points for their lesson. They might privately
choose to focus upon

> 'The voice of my education said to me
> He must be killed'

or    'And immediately I regretted it.'

If the first, then it will be helpful for pupils to
think about the rights and wrongs of killing animals
and our confusion on this issue, and also about how
they have been educated to take moral decisions,
that is, from both direct and indirect experience.
If the second, then it will be helpful to ask pupils
to consider what, uniquely, characterise decision
making which leaves immediate regrets. Here the aim,
clearly, is to arouse their awareness of the inevit-
ability of regret and guilt when there can be no
'right' answer, because of our conflicting emotions
about the competing arguments.

      To summarise, a teacher might choose any one of
the following entries into this poem as a way of
anticipating the complexity of Lawrence's experience,
and of raising pupils' confidence in their ability
to understand and appreciate how Lawrence's language
has realised it.

1.    Elicit pupils' associations with the title
      'snake', and invite accounts of experiences of
      snakes, aiming for expressions of, or awareness
      of, conflicting feelings amongst or within
      themselves.

2.    Explore pupils' attitudes towards man's rela-
      tionship with the living world, especially
      towards animals.

3.    Discuss ways in which we learn how to behave,
      or of how we resolve difficult decisions -
      either to anticipate later class discussion, or
      to provide a starting point for pupils to in-
      vestigate the poem themselves, and then lead
      class discussion on the stages of Lawrence's
      experience.

      Another decision which a teacher must make is
about his explanation of unfamiliar words. We have
found it necessary to explain 'Etna' and 'albatross'
to most classes, desirable to explain 'carob' and
'fissure', and advisable to leave 'expiate' until
pupils can be asked to explain this in the context
of the experience at the close of the poem.
      Teachers who wish to introduce pupils to the
question of 'organisation' early in this work -

bearing in mind that this is frequently included for commentary in examination rubrics - might find it helpful to map out briefly, ahead of a public reading, the four key stages of the poet's experience. The important point with this, as with other 'technical' features, is to find ways of avoiding mere listing and labelling. We hope that, during class discussion, pupils will recognise why our attention is focused first on the snake, and why, then, it is shifted to and fro between the snake and the man, until the creature's undignified disappearance. What we are seeking is their recognition of how this organisation derives from the special nature of the experience, that it is the snake who controls how the man reacts and, to a large extent, that this is what the poem is <u>about</u>. Similarly, over matters of line lengths, repetitions, arresting images, the colloquialisms among the 'poetic' language, we should be trying to stimulate and develop pupils' appreciation of how they express what is happening in the poem. After a public reading of the complete poem, ask pupils to reread silently those lines which introduce the snake.


TEACHER'S QUESTIONS


The First Section

>  A snake came to my water trough
>  ...
>  On the day of Sicilian July, with Etna smoking.

Questions on this section should be phrased to establish, firstly, the intensity of the heat. Ask pupils to decide how we are made aware of the snake's and the man's shared need for water. Lawrence's use of repetition is likely to be promptly mentioned - 'hot', 'hot', 'for the heat' - together with the physical details of place and time. Important, too, is pupils' recognition of the prior claim of the snake. Ask how the poet impresses upon us the snake's arrival at the water before him: the snake is mentioned first; Lawrence states 'I must wait ... he was there before me'. The snake, moreover, is treated first as the man's equal and, soon, as his superior. Ask pupils how we get this impression: not only of course, from 'he' and 'throat', 'mouth' and 'gums', but, suggestively, from 'reached down', 'mused' and 'stooped'. It is helpful for them to be given an opportunity to notice these distinctions because of how they prepare for Lawrence's later perceptions of his snake as a 'god', 'like a king', 'one of the lords of life'. If they are to engage sympathetically with the poet's moral turmoil, pupils need to recognise, early in the poem, the coexistence of 'yellow brown slackness soft bellied' and 'slack long body' with the snake's beauty, dignity and innocence. Lawrence's choice of verbs, his line lengths which suggest leisurely movements, and the associations with harmless 'drinking cattle' are all worth close attention here, if pupils are to understand the ensuing confusion he experiences.

After exploring the opening section, in which Lawrence's fascination with the snake directs his attention to precise details of its appearance, it is valuable to ask one of the class to read it aloud. This can re-establish the mood as well as giving pupils an opportunity to notice additional ways in which the poet has selected and arranged language to re-create his experience: sounds which communicate the delicacy and serenity of the undisturbed snake, say, compared with the undistinguished man, 'in pyjamas for the heat', and the 'drinking cattle'.


## The Second Section

> The voice of my education said to me
> He must be killed
> ...
> From out the dark door of the secret earth.

In these lines we move from the silent, almost spell-bound atmosphere of the physical world to the con-fusion in the poet's mind. Questions on this section should be phrased to elicit expressions of pupils' recognition of the nature of Lawrence's confusion, the exact nature of his dilemma.

What kind of knowledge does he have of this snake so far?

What kind of knowledge urges him to destroy it?

How, apart from his direct statements, does he communicate uncertainty and indecision?

In this section the early personification of the snake as 'he' has been developed through 'guest', 'honoured' and 'hospitality', to communicate the strength of one of the poet's conflicting feelings. By what other means is conflict conveyed and how is his keen anxiety reinforced? By now many pupils have

become familiar with and confident about both the
personification and the repetitions. They might be
asked, also, about the effects upon us, in this
section, of 'taking a stick' and 'finish him off' as
the voices' interpretation of being 'a man'. Why
would it be 'cowardice' not to kill the snake, and
what, precisely, at this point is Lawrence afraid
of?

## The Third Section

> He drank enough
> ...
> Overcame me now his back was turned

The poem returns to the unwary snake, focusing again
on its dignity. Almost hypnotised, Lawrence describes the snake's preparations for departure. How,
pupils can be asked, do we know from the language he
chooses, and how it is arranged, what the snake's
effect upon him is here. What conflicting features
impress him? The personification is extended into
'god' here. Why? What kind of god? 'lifted his head';
'lick his lips'; 'slowly proceeded'. How, though, are
we made aware that the snake is, at the same time, a
sinister animal? 'forked night on the air, so black';
'dreadful hole', 'horrid black hole'. Once the
snake's 'back was turned' the poet's fascination
and uncertainty turn to 'horror', 'a sort of protest'.
Why? Pupils' reponses at this point have convinced
us of the value of spending time on the details of
the early sections of this poem. They have ranged
from the most obvious - that the man's education
has told him that poisonous snakes should be killed;
or that he does not wish to think of himself as a
coward, to the perceptive - that it is his way of
expressing anger that such a rare and beautiful
animal should retreat into such an ugly place (black
hole); anger that this regal creature should appear
to reject him and blithely turn his back on him;
that by returning to the earth, the snake had
started to become 'just a snake again'. There are
few difficulties about pupils' recognition of the
continued indignity of the man - from 'pyjamas for
the heat'; 'take a stick'; 'finish him off' to
'now his back was turned', and of how this is
developed in the final section.

## The Fourth Section

    I think it did not hit him;
    ...
    A pettiness.

Here is, firstly, a description of several physical
activities. What has caused them? How are we made
aware that they are unattractive? Invite pupils to
compare our view of the snake here - 'part of him
that was left behind convulsed in undignified haste/
writhed like lightning', with the opening section.
Why does Lawrence regret throwing the clumsy log?
When, and only when, is the snake reinstated as 'a
king', 'a king in exile', 'the lord of life'? For
some pupils it might be possible to relate what is
happening here to the Mariner's redemption through
his 'gush of love' for the water snakes. If not, it
should, nevertheless, be possible for them to
realise that only after Lawrence has condemned himself and wished for the snake's return, that is,
trusted his first, powerful feelings instead of his
second hand knowledge, does the snake's mystery and
dignity return. Why, they can be asked, does he
perceive the snake as 'a lord of life'?
    What we hope to have achieved by this lesson,
with its directed introduction and questions, is
pupils' understanding of the complexity of the
poem's experience. Moreover, we hope that, if the
teacher has made a selection of only a very few
technical features which Lawrence employs to re-
create this encounter, pupils will recognise their
purpose at different stages of the experience. At
this early point in pupils' close reading of imaginative literature it is to be hoped that teachers
will limit attention to very few 'technical'
features - organisation, personification and repetition - in this poem. Pupils can, without difficulty, recognise the relationship between the
order in which events happen in this poem and the
central point that it is the snake who determines
everything which occurs, especially if they have
thought about the poem's title. Similarly, they can
see why Lawrence personifies the snake - 'he';
'someone'; 'guest'; 'god'; 'king'. And, finally,
because this encounter seems unbearably long for the
fearful and indecisive poet, the special nature of
each tense moment is recreated through the repetitions.
    Whilst sympathising with teachers who hesitate
to impose their readings of literature upon pupils

and draw back from directed discussions such as I
have described, I am suggesting that these might be
valuable in the very early stages of this work. If
pupils have had many opportunities to develop confidence about expressing their responses to poetry
and prose earlier in the school and to express these
with reference to writers' selection and arrangement of language, they can be asked to volunteer
observations directly after a public reading or
after private study before group discussions. As I
have indicated in the previous section, the evidence
of examination answers suggests that too little
guidance may have been given in this area and that
many might benefit from greater direction, at least
in the early weeks of the Advanced level course.
After that, the most helpful approach is to adopt a
variety of strategies as the course progresses.


ACTIVITIES FOR PUPILS

Experienced teachers will have discovered that,
in the early stages of pair and small group discussion, pupils are helped by being given specific
questions to consider. Teachers might compile work
sheets based upon the questions outlined above for
pupils' guidance, that is, a selection of questions
about the poem's setting, the impressions made by
the snake, the poet's changing moods, the reasons
for his decision to throw the log and for his
immediate regret. Less heavily directive, teachers
might select statements from the poem for pupils to
consider and explain. After several silent readings
pupils might be asked to focus upon 'The voice of
my education said to me/He must be killed' and to
discuss why the poet experiences conflicting
emotions. Or they might reflect upon 'And immediately I regretted it', asking themselves about why he
felt so guilty. They are being asked to consider
what these statements 'mean' in the context of the
whole poem and to try to understand how they are
related. If pupils are judged ready to pursue un-
directed  discussion they can be given copies of
the poem to read silently, or to listen to chosen
readers; they can be asked to prepare notes on what
they believe to be its central experience. After
fifteen or twenty minutes, appointed speakers can
be invited to present summaries of agreement and
disagreement and to formulate questions and problems
expressed by members of his group.
  Pupils can also be asked to prepare public

readings which communicate their understanding of the whole encounter. Teachers who have introduced questions of speaker and audience, mood, shifts in place and time, and familiarised pupils with the effects of pacing, pauses and emphasis, can ask them to jot down 'director's notes' to the chosen readers. If the whole group is asked, in pairs or small groups, to work on the same poem for eventual public readings, pupils' interpretations can provide the starting points for class discussion.

Finally, teachers might consider the opportunities which creative writing offers for pupils to show the quality of their individual response. After reading 'Snake' they might be asked either to write about an encounter with an animal which created uncertainties for them, or, leading from their recognition of the difficulty of making decisions in complex situations, to write from the starting point of 'immediately I regretted it'.

NOTES

1. Peter Clough, 'Speaking and Listening: Coming to Know', English Studies 11-18, An Arts Based Approach, edited by Bernard T. Harrison (Hodder and Stoughton, London, 1983) pp. 19-20.
2. D.H. Lawrence 'Snake' Birds, Beasts and Flowers (Martin Secker, London, 1923), pp. 113-116.

## II

### NOVEMBER

The month of the drowned dog. After long rain the land
Was sodden as the bed of an ancient lake,
Treed with iron and birdless. In the sunk lane
The ditch – a seep silent all summer –

Made brown foam with a big voice: that, and my boots
On the lane's scrubbed stones, in the gulleyed leaves,
Against the hill's hanging silence;
Mist silvering the droplets on the bare thorns

Slower than the change of daylight.
In a let of the ditch a tramp was bundled asleep:
Face tucked down into beard, drawn in
Under its hair like a hedgehog's. I took him for dead,

But his stillness separated from the death
Of the rotting grass and the ground. A wind chilled,
And a fresh comfort tightened through him,
Each hand stuffed deeper into the other sleeve.

His ankles, bound with sacking and hairy band,
Rubbed each other, resettling. The wind hardened;
A puff shook a glittering from the thorns,
And again the rains' dragging grey columns

Smudged the farms. In a moment
The fields were jumping and smoking; the thorns
Quivered, riddled with the glassy verticals.
I stayed on under the welding cold

Watching the tramp's face glisten and the drops on his coat
Flash and darken. I thought what strong trust
Slept in him – as the trickling furrows slept,
And the thorn-roots in their grip on darkness;

And the buried stones, taking the weight of winter;
The hill where the hare crouched with clenched teeth.
Rain plastered the land till it was shining
Like hammered lead, and I ran, and in the rushing wood

Shuttered by a black oak leaned.
The keeper's gibbet had owls and hawks
By the neck, weasels, a gang of cats, crows:
Some, stiff, weightless, twirled like dry bark bits


In the drilling rain. Some still had their shape,
Had their pride with it; hung, chins on chests,
Patient to outwait these worst days that beat
Their crowns bare and dripped from their feet.

TED  HUGHES

Approaches to Poems

I have chosen to consider this poem next for reasons
similar to those which I gave for the choice of
'Snake' to open this section. Its content, or subject matter - a re-creation of the poet's responses
to events in the natural world - is likely to be
readily accessible to all sixth formers. After re-
flecting upon and identifying the special quality of
November's damp landscape, pupils are likely to be
able to understand the poet's thoughts and feelings
on encountering the sleeping tramp and the dead
animals. Like Lawrence, Hughes addresses the reader
directly, which delays pupils' difficulties for the
time being with questions about relations between
writer and speaker, and audiences inside and outside
the poem. Very little vocabulary is unfamiliar; we
have found that only 'let', 'seep' and, sometimes,
'gibbet' need explanation. More importantly, close
consideration of 'November', after the experience of
Lawrence's poetry, can develop and reinforce pupils'
awareness of two 'stylistic' or 'technical' features.
As in 'Snake', attention is focused firstly upon the
landscape and then upon the poet. If pupils have
observed and understood how Lawrence's perceptions
of the physical world shaped the whole poem, they
may be prepared to recognise how organisation and
experience are interdependent in 'November'. It is
hoped too that, if they have recognised how repetitions increase the tensions and anxieties in
'Snake' and other Lawrence poems, they can be encouraged to appreciate, by contrast, the effects of
Hughes' grammatical compressions in 'November'. If
they move from the dazzling, breathless heat, from
a landscape where hardly anything stirs, to the
pelting ferocity of winter scenes, pupils may
appreciate how Hughes' choice and arrangement of
language forces multiple impressions simultaneously
upon his readers.

As with the other poems and prose passages in
these sections teachers will select the approaches
they judge most appropriate for their sixth form
groups. I shall first give a detailed account of one
possible kind of lesson, that is, one which includes
a directed introduction and follows a public reading
with a series of questions.

Preparation for a teacher directed class discussion of 'November' is more demanding than for
'Snake' but less so than for the poems by Keats and
Donne which follow. As with Lawrence, there is no
need to give more than a very brief introduction to
the poet and his period. Similarly, there are no
classical or historical allusions and very little

difficult vocabulary. The poem's organisation is, of
course, important and so are its striking 'features
of style' which are probably more difficult for many
pupils to recognise and explain than Lawrence's personification and repetitions. If, however, organisation, or shape, are becoming familiar to pupils as
inseparable from the writer's experience and if they
have been introduced to the simple device of repetition in 'Snake', they ought to be prepared for
some of the similarities and differences to be discovered here.

Lesson preparation, therefore, for a traditional, teacher directed class discussion invites
thought about three main points. Firstly, how to
introduce the poem's 'subject matter' to prepare
pupils most confidently and sympathetically for the
poet's development within the poem, how to invite
responses to November as a time of the year in such
a way as to anticipate how Hughes moves from uncertainty - 'I took him for dead', to spiritual
strength - 'I thought what strong trust slept in
him'. Secondly, the teacher needs to decide how to
divide this poem into 'episodes' for close attention
after the first reading so that pupils' awareness is
sharpened of how exactly it is organised. Finally,
he needs to decide when and how to encourage pupils'
appreciation of how Hughes' choice of figures, and
of grammatical compressions - 'treed with iron', 'a
puff shook a glittering' - re-create his special
response to November's intensity and contradictions.

Characteristically, Hughes writes about conflicting emotions aroused by his experience of the
natural world. His shocking discovery of the sleeping tramp in hostile weather deepens his awareness
of the coexistence of death and renewal in November
and leads him to reflect upon the moral qualities of
living creatures' determination to survive; 'clenched
teeth', 'patient to outwait these worst days'.
The single word title prepares readers for the
poem's concentration upon this month's special
quality, of life in death, beauty in nature's
hostility, drowned dog and shining land, an equili-
brium which Hughes realises with spiritual intensity
- 'bare thorns', 'bound ankles', 'darkening drops',
bare 'crowns' and feet.


INTRODUCTION

Before reading and discussing the poem teachers
might ask pupils about their associations with

November in England. This can give all pupils in
the group some confidence in the poem's access-
ibility and perhaps even a sense of affinity with
the poet. If carefully shaped, a brief explanation
of pupils' experiences can prepare them to recognise
Hughes' keen awareness of the month's contradictions
and the emotions they arouse in him. Begin by asking
about the weather pupils usually expect in November
- cold, wet, windy; about the colours of the English
countryside - black, brown, dull green, grey, silver;
about the sounds most characteristic of this time of
year - wind, rain, storms. It is helpful to focus
upon the special qualities of this time of year, how
it is <u>different</u> from autumn and winter. The countryside often appears to be dying in November - unlike
October which is still colourful and unlike December
and January which are bleak and cold. These opening
enquiries might stimulate pupils' awareness of the
uniqueness of their personal experiences, like or
unlike each other's and Hughes', and sharpen their
sense of the special in-between quality of this time
of year. Once observations about rain storms and
their effects have been expressed, pupils are more
likely to be receptive to the poet's re-creation of
his landscape and the relationships he perceives
between living creatures and the elements.

Introduce the poem, then, as Hughes' attempt to
penetrate the nature of this time of year and to
communicate what it means to him by describing two
unusual experiences whilst walking alone in the
countryside. Some pupils might be helped by being
told before the first reading aloud that the poet
leads gradually towards and away from his discovery
of the tramp and asked to notice how his moods
change. Most groups realise how the scenes change,
and thus how the poem is organised, from how the
teacher separates its 'episodes' for detailed discussion after the first reading aloud. Teachers
always have to decide how helpful pupils are likely
to find being given pointers <u>before</u> reading unfamiliar literature towards the 'features of organisation and style'. Preparation of this lesson
involves thinking about how to anticipate, and
partly overcome, pupils' likely difficulties, without overloading the introduction at the expense of
class discussion.

After the first reading by the teacher, which
pupils follow in their texts, introduce the opening
section, that is, up to line 9, by saying that this
sets the scene, the countryside on a wet November
day, and begin to explore the description through

questions which introduce some of the contradictions
which will be developed throughout the poem. There
are several advantages in paying close attention to
the first three sentences only at the opening of the
discussion. Rereading them familiarises pupils with
a new text. Exploring a small section creates confidence about ways to examine the rest of the poem.
Most importantly, noticing the brevity of the title,
the economical opening statement, the recurrent
ellipsis, the ambiguity, anticipates the later contrasts and the poet's responses to them. It establishes a way of reading.

TEACHER'S QUESTIONS

First Section ll. 1-9

Pupils can be asked firstly to discover everything in this landscape which seems to be dead
- the dog, the trees, the thorns; drowned, iron,
birdless and bare. What, in the same landscape, is
alive? The water in the ditch and, of course, the
poet himself. Apart from the evidence of the poem
itself, how do we know about his and the ditch's
vitality, his awareness of the affinity between
them? The ditch 'makes' foam, and 'my boots', together with this sound, contrast with 'silence'.
Pupils can be asked both about the effects Hughes
seeks in 'treed with iron' and in leaving out the
second verb in his description of 'the ditch' and
'my boots'. Ask them to try to explain what exactly
he is doing here and how it relates to his meaning.
The central point, however, is to establish Hughes'
awareness of the coexistence of death and life in
the same scene, and then to reinforce pupils' recognition of this by asking them about the impression he wants to give of the water. What, thus, is
neither dead, like the dog, nor alive, like the
ditch and the walking man? The whole land is
'sodden', and the mist, contrasting with this ugli-
ness, 'silvers' the droplets. By using the adjective
'slower', Hughes describes the process of the mist
silvering; he suggests both its gentleness and
inexorability.
        Already, therefore, much that is to come -
subject matter, attitude and stylistic features -
can be discovered and expressed in response to
directed questions about the contrasts and Hughes'
economical use of language. The final point to be

considered whilst preparing for class discussion of
this section is the value of introducing observation
of the relationship between the natural and mechanical - 'treed with iron', 'mist silvering the
droplets' - and the religious associations of
'hill's hanging silence' and the 'bare thorns'. Most
pupils are struck immediately by the unusual presence of iron and silver and are ready with suggestions and explanations about their tactile and visual
effects. Few realise until the end of the poem that
Hughes associates the tramp's and animals' endurance
with Christ's patience and humility. This relationship is probably best left for discovery later in
the lesson or during private reading for a directed
homework assignment.

## The Second Section ll. 10-18

Move on to the second episode, from 'In a let of a
ditch' to 'Rubbed each other resettling', in which
Hughes describes his discovery of the sleeping tramp
whom he takes 'for dead'. After rereading these
lines, begin with this reaction and how it is ex-
.pressed, in order to establish the poet's mistake.
Ask pupils again to find the contrasts between death
and life in the whole scene - 'was bundled', 'his
hair', 'rotting grass' suggest decomposition; 'face
tucked in beard', 'stillness', 'fresh comfort',
'ankles rubbed ... resettling' all convey persistent
life. Why is the tramp compared with the hedgehog?
Pupils' responses here can be recalled later when
the class discusses the relationship between the
keeper and the dead birds of prey. In this section
pupils' attention might be drawn to Hughes' various
compressions and they can be asked to explain what
they think are the effects he intends. Which words
(such as 'his' in the first sentence) does he leave
out or alter, and why? How are they arranged un-
usually to sharpen our impressions of the scene?
Ask pupils to look especially at 'A wind chilled'
and 'a fresh comfort tightened through him'. Close
attention reveals the economy with which the poet
communicates a very disturbing experience through
simple and familiar language.

## The Third Section ll. 18-30

The third section, from 'The wind hardened' to 'the
hare crouched with clenched teeth' can, though

complex, be taken with most groups as a whole. Many
pupils, though, find it helpful to explore it in two
parts, firstly looking at Hughes' description of the
worsening weather and then at the poet's involvement
with the tramp and his response both to him and to
the rest of enduring nature. Firstly, focus upon
how Hughes conveys nature's increasing hostility. Look
carefully at 'The wind hardened' to discover exactly
what is happening - its force strengthens, it feels
solid, it hardens those it attacks, rather like the
comfort which 'tightened' against the chill. Look,
too, at the mere 'puff' which shakes 'a glittering',
for how this noun communicates both beauty and the
rain's weight. Ask how Hughes relates the wind and
the rain by 'hardened' and 'grey columns'. If the
farms become smudged and the fields are made to jump
and smoke, if nature is felt to be 'on the offensive'
- 'grey columns', 'smoking', 'riddled' - this must
affect our feelings for the tramp, already recognised as a lonely outcast from the rest of society.
It is helpful to invite pupils' responses, therefore, at this stage, to how the poet communicates
the force of the storm (by his military and indust-
rial imagery and his compressions) and to how this
affects our feelings about the tramp curled up in
the ditch. What precisely intrigues the poet to keep
him 'under the welding cold'? What explains the
change in his feelings, from his confession of a
mistake - 'I took him for dead' into the reflection
'I thought what strong trust slept in him'? Exploration of the ways in which, though beautiful, nature
feels so keenly hostile leads some pupils to volunteer that the tramp is seen almost like a martyr.
They notice 'the drops on his coat flash and darken'
even if they have only weak associations with the
repeated thorns and thorn roots. Most pupils readily
recognise the force of the comparison between
'strong trust' and 'the trickling furrows' and how
all that follows - thorn roots, buried stones, the
hill, the crouching hare - relate the sleeping tramp
with the rest of nature which resists and persists
through winter. What, they can be asked, does Hughes
claim in common between the sleeping tramp and the
rest of nature? Pupils easily recognise the affinities between his serene resignation and the landscape's and animals' endurance, the parallels
between his survival instinct and the persistent
natural life amid the changing seasons. This is the
point, of course, to discuss what they take to be
the meaning of 'trust' which 'sleeps' and how much
Hughes values this trust.

This section gives opportunities for recognising and appreciating figurative language in the
poem's experience - 'dragging grey columns',
'jumping and smoking', 'riddled with glassy verticals', 'welding cold'; and for discussing the poet's
intention in personifying the rain, fields, thorns,
cold and furrows. Together with reflection upon the
four different, though related, subjects of the
verb 'slept', close attention to Hughes' language
reveals its inseparability from his meaning. He has
discovered, and chosen language to communicate this
discovery, that he would be as wrong to take nature
as dead in November as he had been when he took the
tramp 'for dead'. All the verbs - hardened, shook,
smudged, quivered, slept - testify to his keen sense
of their subjects' shared vitality.


## The Fourth Section ll. 31-40

The final episode in 'November' moves in time and
place and redefines the close relationships the poet
perceives within nature. His strengthening sense of
nature's aggression and endurance develops and com-
plicates what he feels November represents for him.
How, pupils can be asked, has the scene changed?
What is the contrast between the first and second
parts of the first sentence? The open 'land' has
given way to 'the rushing wood' and almost homely
protection of the 'shuttered oak'. Which verbs and
adjectives sustain the persistent contrast in the
poem between hostility - 'plastered' and 'hammered'
- and beauty and comfort - 'shining' and 'shuttered'? What does the poet communicate about his
experience of the elements by his choice of 'plastered' and 'rushing'? After rereading this section,
ask pupils how man is shown as part of nature's
destructiveness, also responsible for the presence
of death at this time of the year. Look carefully at
the effect of the list of animals, how it conveys a
large number and, of course, what the animals have
in common as birds of prey. Which word communicates
man's own effectiveness as a killer? Perhaps,
at this point, 'gibbet' will recall associations
with 'hanging hill', the thorns, bound ankles,
sacking and hairy band. Perhaps an invitation to
reflect on our associations with 'drilling', alongside the image of the swinging corpses will suggest
instruments of torture which are as much a part of
man's world as the elements. The main aim here is to
recognise how the choice and arrangement of language

- 'stiff' (like human corpses) and 'bits of dry bark' - suggest parallels with human death and nature's decomposition and communicate Hughes' sense of the network of relationships and contradictions in November's world. Ask pupils to consider the significance of the differences between the corpses - 'some, stiff weightless'; 'some still had their shape' - some are like the trees and some, the wettest, are like the sleeping tramp. Which words remind us of the sleeping tramp? 'Still'; 'Chins on chests'; 'patient to outwait'. The striking word here is 'crowns' and pupils might be asked which of its several associations they think Hughes is suggesting.

Time must be found for a rereading before the end of the lesson. If there is time, it would be valuable to ask pupils to prepare a reading; if not, part of a directed task could be to prepare this for another lesson. The detailed work which remains, if the teacher judges this appropriate for a written exercise, is upon the variety of ellipses in 'November' and upon the poem's sound symbolism. Having been given guidance in class discussion - the single word title, the brevity of the opening sentence, some reflection upon 'treed with iron', 'mist silvering', pupils can be asked to look carefully for omissions and compressions to explain the effects achieved in the descriptions where they occur. Also, since the poem employs recurrent vowels and consonants for a variety of sensuous effects, pupils can be asked to identify and explain these as part of their prepared readings.

Three main suggestions, however, have been made about approaching 'November' for class discussion. Firstly it has been proposed that pupils' knowledge and experience of the season should be elicited and shaped in readiness for the contrasts they will meet in the poem. Secondly that, after the first reading, the poem is discussed in four episodes, each of which is reread before questions are asked. Thirdly it is suggested that questions are organised and phrased to focus firstly upon contrasts and contradictions and then upon the relationships and affinities within the natural world. It is also hoped that some of the recurrent features of Hughes' choice and arrangement of language, especially his figurative language and compressions - which communicate the intensity of his experiences - might be explored so that pupils gain an awareness of the relationship of meaning and style.

ACTIVITIES FOR PUPILS

Some teachers might prefer to offer this poem to
their pupils for individual reflection, or for small
group discussion, as a preliminary to directed
writing or reporting back to the whole class. They
have to decide, in this case, how much guidance is
likely to be appreciated. After a brief introduction
which draws upon the suggested opening to a conventional lesson, teachers can simply distribute copies
of the poem without direction, or can ask one or
several specific questions. As a general guideline
for pupils working on their own teachers might consider asking them to perform for themselves some of
the tasks which would have been included in their
own questions. Pupils might be asked to think about
the poem's title and its relationship with the experience of the poem. They might be asked to consider the impact of the tramp upon the poet and the
tramp's relationship with the animals in the wood –
focusing upon 'I took him for dead' and 'I thought
what strong trust/Slept in him'. They might be asked
whether they think 'November' is a religious poem,
and what is Hughes' view of the natural world.
     Teachers who are interested in increasing
pupils' awareness of how poems are organised might
ask their groups to discuss among themselves how
'November' moves in place, time and mood and to be
prepared to explain how they see its different
'episodes'. Similarly, again drawing upon the
sequence of questions outlined above, they might ask
them to explore Hughes' poem for unusual descriptions and sentences, 'effective irregularities'.
     With confident and experienced pupils who will
not easily lose heart because of their confusion
about the poem's 'meaning', a valuable strategy is
to give ample time for their preparation of public
readings. Pairs or small groups need time to discuss
the poem in detail to arrive at decisions about how
it might be read. Every section confronts them with
decisions about emphasis, raising questions about
sentence structure, weighting of words, and appropriate rhythms. This activity draws pupils' attention to the poet's recurrent compressions and, of
course, to the sound qualities of the language.
Trying out on their tongues and hearing the poet's
words may give pupils' greater confidence to comment
upon aspects of craftsmanship and, gradually, to
recognise its inseparability from meaning.

III


ODE ON MELANCHOLY


No, no, go not to Lethe, neither twist
   Wolf's-bane, tight-rooted, for its poisonous wine;
Nor suffer thy pale forehead to be kiss'd
   By nightshade, ruby grape of Proserpine;
Make not your rosary of yew-berries,
    Nor let the beetle, nor the death-moth be
      Your mournful Psyche, nor the downy owl
A partner in your sorrow's mysteries;
    For shade to shade will come too drowsily,
      And drown the wakeful anguish of the soul.


But when the melancholy fit shall fall
   Sudden from heaven like a weeping cloud,
That fosters the droop-headed flowers all,
   And hides the green hill in an April shroud;
Then glut thy sorrow on a morning rose,
    Or on the rainbow of the salt sand-wave,
      Or on the wealth of globèd peonies;
Or if thy mistress some rich anger shows,
    Emprison her soft hand, and let her rave,
      And feed deep, deep upon her peerless eyes.


She dwells with Beauty - Beauty that must die;
   And Joy, whose hand is ever at his lips
Bidding adieu; and aching Pleasure nigh,
   Turning to poison while the bee-mouth sips:
Ay, in the very temple of Delight
    Veil'd Melancholy has her sovran shrine,
      Though seen of none save him whose strenuous tongue
Can burst Joy's grape against his palate fine;
    His soul shall taste the sadness of her might,
      And be among her cloudy trophies hung.

JOHN KEATS

# Approaches to Poems

I have chosen to present suggestions for a teacher
directed discussion of this poem for several reasons.
It offers opportunities for further recognition of
some of the features which have been introduced
during close reading of the first two poems: clearly,
how Keats chooses to organise his reflections on
melancholy is worth detailed attention; unlike
'November', but like 'Snake', Keats' subject here is
personified as a deity; again the poem's imagery is
very striking, especially in the way it carries
forward and enriches the argument. This ode is
obviously different from the first two poems in
several important ways and therefore introduces new
decisions for teachers in the early stages of this
work. This poem could be many sixth formers' first
experience of literature written before this century
and their first encounter with a poet's attempt to
penetrate the exact nature of a mood or season in
this form. The ode faces teachers with the need to
find a way of dealing with the classical allusions,
without an understanding of which much of the poem
is incomprehensible. They have to decide how much to
explain before the poem is read and discussed and
who is to provide the explanation. Lastly, this ode
introduces pupils to further ways in which imagery
features in poetry, that is, to the special richness
of the sensuous experience of taste.

On each of these new points decisions need to
be taken about when, how and by whom the explanations and introductions are best given to the group.
In our experience sixth formers at the beginning of
an Advanced level course gain most confidence about
the sense they can make of poetry when their difficulties with unfamiliar allusions and vocabulary
have been cleared up. It seems sensible, therefore,
for teachers to anticipate these difficulties and
either to give explanations themselves or direct
pupils to provide them for the class before the
first public reading. Lethe, Proserpine and Psyche
will be unfamiliar. We have discovered, too, that
few pupils in urban schools know what wolf's bane,
nightshade and even peonies are. Whilst some will
hazard that nightshade and yew berries are poisonous,
we have rarely found many who can describe what they
look like or where they grow. Teachers will choose
what they think are the most appropriate ways of
overcoming this difficulty - glossaries, pictures
of wild and garden flowers, pupil searches before
the lesson in classical and botanical dictionaries.
The point is that this ode, like many poems,
especially written in earlier periods, will need

consideration of how to provide the background material to leave pupils free to make contributions
without unnecessary and discouraging misinterpretations.

## INTRODUCTION

It may be worth spending time upon the title and
upon giving a very brief outline of how the poem is
organised. Some teachers will prefer their pupils to
discover what melancholy is during their experience
of the poem. By asking pupils what they think melancholy is, however, and when we are most likely to
experience it, a way can be found of anticipating
Keats' search for times which arouse both delight
and despair. Pupils usually equate melancholy with
depression and sadness. They can become intrigued by
the notion of exploring and attempting to re-create
chosen experiences when these are most keenly felt.
Asked to consider when we are most likely to be sad,
when the mood might be at its most intense, pupils
frequently offer from their own experiences those
which come close to Keats' response to the short-
lived nature of beauty and joy. Pupils themselves
therefore can provide ways into their recognition
and appreciation of the contrasts between the first
and second stanzas. A brief time spent considering
the meaning of melancholy as a preliminary to the
first public reading can also serve to introduce
this poem's organisation. Pupils can usefully be
told, before the first reading, that the poem consists of three distinct, but related sections, three
long sentences. If this is to be a teacher directed
lesson, early in their course, they can be greatly
helped by knowing that the first describes those
experiences Keats rejects, the second those which he
urges us to accept and that the last contains his
explanation or conclusion. Their responsibility,
whilst following the reading and looking again
privately at the poem, is to notice what exactly
characterise the experiences in stanzas one and two
and how they are communicated.

## TEACHER'S QUESTIONS

### First Stanza 11. 1-10

After the first public and private readings, a
teacher directed lesson will probably concentrate

upon each stanza separately. Questions will be
phrased and sequenced to encourage pupils' confidence in their ability to discern meaning and to
relate to it the poet's choice and arrangement of
language. Questions on the first stanza will be
phrased in such a way as to prepare for pupils' own
recognition of how this stanza contrasts with the
second. If teachers succeed in stimulating pupils'
awareness of everything about those experiences
which Keats rejects, they might have sharpened
pupils' appreciation of all the contrasts, the
positives, which follow. Ask pupils to look for
what the experiences have in common in the first
stanza, giving them a few moments to look at it
again privately and to hear it re-read. If they are
asked, too, to consider how he addresses the reader
- 'go not', 'nor suffer', 'make not', 'nor let' -
they will establish early the strength of his
rejection. If, with an inexperienced group, a
teacher thinks it would be helpful, he will ask
pupils to notice where these experiences take place
(underground and in churchyards) and when (at night
time and in darkness). Pupils who are encouraged to
notice and reflect upon this are likely to be able
to explain why Keats urges the reader away from
these extreme experiences; they are in a stronger
position to notice the effect of 'wakeful' in the
stanza's final line.


## Second Stanza 11. 11-20

Now fully prepared for Keats' move, his 'But when
...', into those experiences  he feels are more intensely and richly sad, pupils can be asked to look
closely at the simile he chooses for the 'melancholy
fit'. How, firstly, is a 'fit' different from the
sorrowful experiences described in the first stanza?
Most pupils, given time to think about this, recognise the contrast between the effects of drugs
and poison and those of a passing mood. What are all
the other differences, about place and time? The
image of an April shower and its associations is, of
course, central to Keats' complex perception of
melancholy as a reviving experience: the cloud might
weep, the flowers might droop, the hill be hidden in
a shroud, but the rain is nourishing, the flowers
will bloom again as April is followed by summer. It
is worth spending time on this simile alone for a
few moments in order for pupils to explore their
responses to these natural images. We hope that this

will give them the opportunity to discover the interrelationship Keats is suggesting between changes in
the natural world and our own responses to life,
once we have come to recognise the inextricability
of sadness and joy. This simile invites reflection
because it is central to Keats' redefinition of
melancholy as an active experience; it prepares the
reader for Keats' instruction to 'glut' and 'feed'
upon experiences of transient beauty. When, therefore, is he suggesting that sadness is experienced
most keenly? What have the experiences he directs us
to, in common? Where, firstly, are they to be found?
And when? Why does Keats choose 'glut' and 'feed'?
How does his enthusiasm for excess here differ from
the extremes in the opening stanza?

### Third Stanza 11. 21-30

Most pupils find the final stanza straightforward.
They will have met personifications already and
accept readily Keats' statements here about dying
beauty, departing joy and painful pleasure. The
focal questions here are, of course, about the kind
of man who is capable of experiencing melancholy
fully - the 'strenuous tongue' and 'palate fine' and
about the reverence Keats wishes to communicate for
the emotion through the religious imagery.
    The main feature of Keats' poem which most
sixth form teachers will probably want to introduce
is the celebrated richness of its imagery. Some
might decide to prepare for the odes by bringing in
a few verses of 'The Eve of Saint Agnes' for pupils'
enjoyment of his descriptive powers. It might be
valuable for pupils to read this first for the
vividness and detail with which it conveys sensuous
qualities.

> And still she slept an azure-lidded sleep,
> In blanchèd linen, smooth and lavender'd,
> While he from forth the closet brought a heap
> Of candied apple, quince, and plum, and gourd;
> With jellies soother than the creamy curd,
> And lucent syrops, tinct with cinnamon.

Here the imagery serves a straightforward
descriptive purpose, whilst in the ode pupils can be
invited to recognise how it is part of the poem's
argument. Some teachers might approach pupils'
consideration of Keats' imagery in this ode by
taking the phrase 'palate fine', either as part of

their introduction or at some stage of pupils' close reading of the poem. Ask pupils to think about the senses involved in wine tasting, and about the kind of person who is most likely to enjoy this activity. Why might he be chosen as a way of communicating the special qualities involved in responding fully to life's experiences? How does Keats' choice of such a person unite the various parts of this poem? ('Wolf's bane' ... 'poisonous wine'; 'burst joy's grape')

Rereadings, of single lines or groups of lines, complete stanzas and complete poems, are extremely valuable at every stage of this work in the sixth form. Hopefully, teachers will try to vary their approaches between requests for silent readings and invitations to pairs and small groups of pupils to prepare public readings for class comment and queries. Pupils can reasonably be asked, as they become more familiar with a poem, to try to be observant about its sound values and their purpose: 'tight-rooted', 'ruby', 'yew-berries'; 'weeping', 'green', 'peonies', 'feed deep', 'peerless'. How have these been arranged and how do they relate to 'meaning'? When, as here, a poem is an address, there are additional questions of attitude to be considered when preparing a public reading – the poet's situation, his approach to his subject or problem, and his approach to his readers.


ACTIVITIES FOR PUPILS

Most teachers of new sixth formers who choose to introduce this poem for close reading are likely to decide to conduct traditional class discussion in which they play a leading part. Anticipating their pupils' unfamiliarity with its vocabulary, not only the classical and botanical references, but also 'melancholy', 'rosary' and 'peerless', they will wish to avoid their pupils' possible discouragement and confusion upon being asked to respond to something which, even after several readings, means very little without considerable help.

This might be an occasion, therefore, on which to suggest that teachers and pupils share the work on the poem. After having been given explanations by teachers of most of the unfamiliar vocabulary and guidelines on how the poem is organised, and listened to a public reading, pupils can be asked to look, in close detail, at each stanza and to jot down their impressions. They might be asked to note their impressions of the settings, especially the colours, in the first two stanzas. What, as they read, especially aloud to each other, do they see, hear, touch, taste and smell, imaginatively, in these descriptions - the root, grape, berry, beetle, moth and owl; and, then, the spring countryside, the sea-shore, the garden of peonies and the love scene? After impressions have been exchanged - and areas of difference explored - pupils can be asked to address themselves to the poem's argument, to working through Keats' 'instructions' to the reader.

When pupils have had time to recognise the poem's three sentences, how they are constructed and how they relate, they can be asked to prepare their own public readings which communicate what they believe to be the mood of each section. This is the point at which pupils begin to hear how the sounds are part of the experiences of the images, how Lethe and beetle, rooted, ruby and yew, are part of the torpor which Keats rejects; and how fit, fall, foster and flowers, and rose, rainbow and globed are part of the beauty he embraces.

Pupils in the early, and even the middle, years at school are often invited to illustrate poems. Some sixth form teachers enrich their pupils' experience of English at this level by encouraging them to produce collages and other illustrations. Taking in prints of Guernica during work on The Waste Land for Advanced level, students have been excited and impressed by sets of collages produced by pupils in response to T.S. Eliot's poem - patterns composed from cut-outs, their own drawings, photographs, snippets of scores. On becoming increasingly confident about their understanding of The Waste Land, and stimulated by its variety of voices and cultures, pupils successfully communicated their powers of observation, their involvement and the quality of their responses through what they chose and how they arranged their chosen fragments. Some teachers might invite pupils' visual responses to Keats' Ode, might invite them to communicate their interpretation of the experiences he describes by re-creating them visually - river, hedgerow, ditches, churchyard, and the contrasting spring countryside, seashore and gardens.

IV

A VALEDICTION : forbidding mourning

As virtuous men passe mildly away,
    And whisper to their soules, to goe,
Whilst some of their sad friends doe say,
    The breath goes now, and some say, no:

So let us melt, and make no noise,
    No teare-floods, nor sigh-tempests move,
T'were prophanation of our joyes
    To tell the layetie our love.

Moving of th'earth brings harmes and feares,
    Men reckon what it did and meant,
But trepidation of the spheares,
    Though greater farre, is innocent.

Dull sublunary lovers love
    (Whose soule is sense) cannot admit
Absence, because it doth remove
    Those things which elemented it.

But we by a love, so much refin'd,
    That our selves know not what it is,
Inter-assured of the mind,
    Care lesse, eyes, lips, and hands to misse.

Our two soules therefore, which are one,
    Though I must goe, endure not yet
A breach, but an expansion,
    Like gold to ayery thinnesse beate.

If they be two, they are two so
    As stiffe twin compasses are two,
Thy soule the fixt foot, makes no show
    To move, but doth, if the'other doe.

And though it in the center sit,
    Yet when the other far doth rome,
It leanes, and hearkens after it,
    And growes erect, as that comes home.

Such wilt thou be to mee, who must
    Like th'other foot, obliquely runne;
Thy firmnes makes my circle just,
    And makes me end, where I begunne.

JOHN DONNE

103

I have included a seventeenth century poem in this group because it appears to be standard practice for many English teachers to introduce Donne's poetry in their practical criticism courses and because of the special problems which this presents. At their least successful teachers tend to give too much 'background' or too little. Common sense directs the majority to give some preliminary information, verbally or in handouts, about 'metaphysical poetry', 'conceits', and 'wit', whilst those who justifiably fear the likely discouragement this produces, try to raise pupils' awareness of what these mean during class discussion. In my view Donne's poem needs some initial preparation and, once again, I suggest that teachers think very carefully about how a reasonable balance might be struck between asking and telling, and between the work they and the pupils do both on the introduction and on the complete poem.

This poem differs in several ways from those we have already considered. Consequently, thought needs to be given to how pupils might most confidently grasp these new features, most especially as they characterise a different cultural and intellectual climate from the earlier poems. Firstly, since it is a dramatic address, part of a conversation, the poem invites consideration of the speaker's and listener's identities. Here, unlike the poets Lawrence, Hughes and Keats, Donne is speaking as lover, with a particular audience, his beloved, whom he addresses throughout the poem. Lawrence, Hughes, and Keats through his personification, Melancholy, were addressing unspecified, hopefully responsive, readers in the outside world 'out there' as Seamus Heaney said on a recent television programme. Donne, as his title indicates, addresses an audience inside his poem. It is, in a special sense, more private and intimate than the others, not only because of what the argument asserts about the nature of his and his mistress' relationship, but because of how it is conducted. This poem is one side of a conversation. The language is mostly simple, the expressions almost colloquial - 'some of their sad friends'; 'what it did and meant' - and, because the poet/speaker/lover is conducting an argument, the poem is organised very differently from the earlier ones. The title, the identity of the speaker, the precise situation in which the address is made, all help to explain how sentences are structured to move on this argument - 'as' and 'so' and 'but' and 'if'. Finally, and also related to the dramatic, conversational features of Donne's love and religious poetry, persistent contrasts are employed as ways of exploring the central issue, the mystery of 'a love, so much refin'd/That our selves know not what it is', that is, the celebrated 'wit', which has not been considered so far.

## INTRODUCTION

As a preliminary to a teacher directed lesson or pupil initiated discussion some pupils can be asked to prepare brief informative statements about seventeenth century cosmology, paying particular attention to beliefs about the spheres. Others might do the same for the contemporary metal working processes, with special reference to the melting of gold and the purposes for which it was beaten to 'ayery thinness'. Others might be given the task of looking up the meaning of conceits in literary terminology and presenting to the group some examples of traditional conceits which had become overworked in the seventeenth century. They could find more examples of 'teare floods and sigh-tempests', especially from Shakespeare's plays with which the group might be familiar. It might be helpful for these pupils to contribute some examples of love song cliches which everyone recognises today.

A confident sense of what metaphysical poetry is like and in what wit consists is more likely to be developed from close reading than from opening lectures or handouts. Some time, however, must be given to pupils' or teachers' explanations of a selection of vocabulary and allusions upon which appreciation of this poem depends. With a little help most pupils can cope with 'prophanation' and 'laiety', but most lower sixth formers are unlikely to have any understanding of 'trepidation of the spheares'. It is always worth eliciting information which they already possess: can historians comment upon the main upheavals taking place in the seventeenth century? Can anyone interested in astronomy explain the significance of the rejection of the Ptolemaic for the Copernican theory of the universe? Whilst something will be forthcoming on these points in many sixth forms, it is likely that someone will have to explain that 'trepidation of the spheares' is a seventeenth century version of the precession of the equinoxes; 'trepidation', therefore, might be viewed as 'greater farre' than local earthquakes. What follows now is a proposed outline for a teacher directed lesson which attempts to achieve a reasonable balance between asking and telling. Once again, this is given in detail because, unlike the other suggested strategies, it depends heavily upon the sequence and phrasing of the teacher's questions.

As I have stressed throughout it is worth spending a few moments on the title. What exactly is a valediction? The words used when bidding farewell. This is important, not only to remove confusion, but to establish that the poem is addressed to someone special in a precise situation. When, furthermore, do we 'mourn'? And how does 'forbidding' fit into this? This brief exploration might anticipate some of the poem's tensions between mock seriousness and intensity, the tough-mindedness of the love it explores. Additionally, I suggest that teachers at least consider telling pupils, before the first public reading, that what they are about to meet is a recreation of a lover's instruction to his mistress or wife upon parting. We have observed that some pupils, without the benefit of a preamble about the title or the situation, fail to grasp what is happening at the beginning of this poem, assuming that it is a description of the death bed of the person he is forbidden to mourn. We have rarely been convinced of the value of leaving these pupils in confusion and proceeding to conduct the ensuing discussion with the few who have grasped the significance of the opening sentence without help. Either explore the title, or phrase the first question in such a way that includes the chosen simile, in the early stages of a course which is encouraging close reading.

TEACHER'S QUESTIONS

## The First Section ll. 1-8

After following the teacher's reading pupils can be asked to read over the first two stanzas by themselves, given a few moments to consider the effects of the death bed simile. Why does the speaker choose to compare the lovers' parting with the death of virtuous men? What is it about such deaths that he wishes to characterise their parting? Ask pupils to identify those words which convey the special quality of these particular death beds - 'mildly'; 'whisper'; 'sad'. What does the uncertainty suggest, about death itself, and about the relationship between dying men and 'their sad friends'? How does

Donne suggest that most lovers part? What kind of
lovers might behave like this? Apart from associat-
ing their leavetaking with virtuous men's deaths,
how does Donne communicate the superiority of their
love to the great majority? How else does he raise
it above the level of ordinary human experience?
What is it about conventional lovers' behaviour that
would make it a profanity for Donne and his mistress
to give public expression to their feelings?

If some time has been spent upon the meaning and
implications of this poem's title the question of
relationship between speaker and audience will have
been introduced and can therefore be carried over
into the instructions and assertions in the poem
itself. Pupils can be invited to explore the special
nature of the lovers' relationship and how the
poet's insistence upon privacy and dignity arises
out of this. By what means, they can be asked, does
Donne suggest intimacy, that is, write as if what he
is asking is meant to be part of a conversation?

Perhaps, even at this early stage, especially if
there is time to discuss several of Donne's poems,
the question of what distinguishes this from prose
can be raised. Although this poem is an argument, a
dramatic address written in a diction modelled on
the rough give and take of actual speech, it is
arranged on the page in conventional poetic form.
Many teachers prefer to pursue poems' meaning right
through before returning to examine technique.
Since this might account for many pupils' tendency
to simply label and list technicalities, it might be
more valuable to proceed very slowly through the
opening lines, raising awareness of just a few
'poetic' devices through which the experience is
communicated. Observation of the interrelationship
between a poem's experience and the language chosen
to communicate it in an opening line, a first stanza
or group of verses might make it easier to read the
rest of the poem with closer attention. This poem,
which opens with an extended simile, offers opportunities for pupils to notice other 'poetic'
features which extend and reinforce the associations
intended with virtuous men's death beds. They might
notice how the rhymes function as part of the comparison and contrast which interest the speaker -
goe and noe; noise and joyes. Additionally, especially
after rereading aloud, pupils will probably recognise how Donne's choice of words for sound effects
help to create a hushed, reverent atmosphere. After
a detailed exploration like this some teachers might
prefer pupils to continue close reading at their own

pace, make jottings and report back orally or write individually about what is taking place for a home-work assignment.

## The Second Section 11. 9-20

If the lesson is to proceed through teacher directed class discussion, what next needs to be noticed is the relationship between stanzas three and four and the opening of the poem. What have conventional lovers' public expressions of grief led Donne to think of in the physical world? Why does he choose trepidation of the spheres to distinguish his love from theirs? What exactly distinguishes these trepidations from other terrifying and destructive natural events? At this point it might be helpful if pupils were asked to attempt prose versions of verse three which bring out the distinction between 'moving of th'earth' and 'trepidation of the spheares' and 'men reckon' and 'is innocent'. It will have become obvious that some preliminary information, however brief, needs to have been discovered, or given, about seventeenth century cosmology for pupils to follow how Donne develops his series of contrasts to illustrate the difference in quality between his and ordinary love relationships. Without this they miss not only the seriousness and intensity with which he asserts their superiority. They miss also the oppor-tunity to notice, as many do, that Donne, taking a 'forbidding' stance in the title, like Hamlet out-doing Laertes at Ophelia's grave, introduces un-certainty in his most extreme statements. Moreover, after 'forbidding', 'prophanation' and 'trepidation of the spheares', the simplicity of 'our selves know not what it is' is seen to be more moving in its acceptance of the mystery of personal affinities. What, pupils can be asked, makes other lovers 'dull'? How else, through the language he chooses, does Donne diminish physical love in this stanza? There is an almost cloddish impression here which comes from 'dull', 'sublunary', 'things', 'it'.

## The Third Section 11. 16-30

After being given an opportunity to think about the argument and the sound of this verse, pupils will be ready to move to the second half of the poem. Either the teacher's introduction to the overall organisa-tion of the poem or their own rereadings will have anticipated the turn of 'But we ...', that is, the move into Donne's attempt to explore what exactly happens when their relationship has to undergo physical separation. What are the likely meanings of 'refined', and how is refinement achieved in love between the sexes? How, from the rhymes, does Donne reinforce his own view of this? What does he claim about their love which explains its earlier comparison with virtuous men's deaths and the trepidation of the spheres? How do lovers 'inter-assured of the mind' differ from those whose 'soul is sense'?

Once the special quality of the poet's/speaker's love, which is independent of physical presence, has been established, and his attitude towards it articulated, pupils are ready to appreciate the arresting images ahead and to attempt explanations of why these particularly might have been chosen. They can be invited to pursue the two-in-one paradox, to notice that while the word 'two' persistently recurs, it is inside images which deny or reconcile actual separation. In spite of the repeated 'two's' and verbs of motion, how does Donne succeed in creating a sense of repose and confidence?

Obviously there is still much detailed analysis which can be made of this poem and many teachers will wish to ask for this in addition to, or instead of, preparation of public readings. If they are especially interested in encouraging pupil's observation of imagery, they will ask them to look at it again to identify its images and to comment upon them as they function as exploration of Donne's experience. How, they will ask pupils to consider, do death beds, religion, natural disasters, chemistry and mathematics relate to the experience of love between the sexes? If they are especially interested in pupils' awareness of organisation and arrangement of language in poems, they might ask them to look at how the argument is conducted here, the structure of the sentences, how they extend across the stanzas or are completed within them. Or they might be interested in pupils' recognition of how contrasts are introduced and handled and in relating the contrasts in this poem to the question of 'wit'.

Teachers have to decide, after a class discussion along the lines which I have described, how long to spend on a poem which has become familiar. Rather than pursue too much in one poem, it might be more valuable to ask pupils to read, on their own, a new poem very close in spirit and technique to the one they have discussed in detail. When pupils' confidence has been raised about what to expect and how

to look closely at this kind of poetry, they can be
given a selection of Donne's work, addressed to his
mistress, an intruding friend, God, or to himself,
to prepare themselves to read aloud to the class or
to prepare responses for general class discussion.


ACTIVITIES FOR PUPILS

Several activities have already been suggested
which involve teachers and pupils working on this
poem. Pupils can undertake a variety of tasks before
the poem is discussed in class. They can also work
on their own or in small groups at different stages
of the poem, once directed and specific questions
have been introduced. Additionally, they can be
asked, at these different stages, how the lines
should be spoken and to be prepared to explain their
interpretations.

According to their group's confidence and experience teachers will select an appropriate strategy for encouraging understanding and appreciation
of this poem. Of the poems considered so far this
invites pupils' presentation of public readings.
After class discussion of the precise meaning of its
title, and explanations of unfamiliar vocabulary,
pupils can be given half a period or a homework to
prepare readings which introduce class discussions
about interpretations. Questions of age and sex of
speaker and listener can be raised as preliminaries
to pupils' exploration of the poet's attitude towards their love and towards other people. How confident, pupils can be asked, are Donne's claims for
the lovers' unity in separation? Pupils can be asked
to pay special attention to how the differently constructed sentences communicate the changing moods in
the poem. Ask them to interpret it by how they read
it, that is, re-create the changing moods within the
dramatic address. Can the listeners distinguish the
various stages through which the speaker moves, the
conspiratorial, assertive, uncertain and exploratory,
confident, from the attention readers have given to
organisation, continuities, pauses, rhymes and
repetitions?

A further strategy might be to ask pupils to
look at how the poem is organised. They could offer
a simple prose statement of each stage of the argument and then return to his poem to examine the
additional 'meanings' communicated by the associations and sounds of the language. Either pupils or
teacher can present something like this list:

Let us part without undignified emotional fuss.
Ordinary love cannot tolerate separation.
Our love is different and therefore can
survive partings.

Pupils can be asked to discover all the appositions
within the poem and to be prepared to explain why
they have been chosen and how they think they add,
either to a prose version or to other protestations
of love which the teacher might present from love
poems of other periods or popular lyrics of today.
For some pupils a valuable exercise might be
to put themselves into the place of the person addressed in this poem, the lover who has been forbidden to mourn. As a way of getting more deeply into
the dramatic situation and of showing their awareness of the various levels on which the problem of
parting is being considered, pupils can be asked to
compose a poem or letter in reply. To engage with
the speaker of this valediction, to agree or dis-
agree with his analysis and assertions, those who
attempt a reply need to develop a keen sense of the
person with whom they are involved. Before engaging
in the dialogue from their own perspective, they
will have to be confident, not only about what is
being said, but what it reveals about the speaker
himself.

Chapter Six

APPROACHES TO PROSE: LESSON MATERIAL

Many English teachers find prose passages more
difficult than poetry to prepare for Paper Three at
Advanced level. Their uncertainties derive partly
from the problems we considered in the first section:
how to encourage pupils' personal responses and to
introduce them to the technical analysis apparently
required by examiners' demands for a 'critical
essay' 'critical appreciation' and evidence of
'critical powers' in their rubrics; how to cope with
pupils' unfamiliarity with literature outside their
own period; how to handle pupils' ignorance of traditional grammar and critical terminology. Prose
presents additional problems. Even when taken from
the openings of novels, prose passages are less self
contained than poems. They raise, moreover, in a
more complex fashion than much poetry, the question
of relationship between writer/narrator and audience/
reader. And because most pupils' reading material in
and outside school is prose, systematic discussion
of prose passages appears to be a more awkward and
artificial process than the analysis of poetry.
     As I have already indicated, some teachers
choose to avoid regular preparation of their pupils
for the 'unseen', except for analysis of the set
texts. Others organise rigorous programmes of work
on technical features - diction, imagery, figurative
language, rhetorical devices and sentence structures.
Teachers using some of the currently available texts
in this area are likely to take their pupils through
prose style, either chronologically - with examples
from different periods of English literature -
or technically, identifying features of style and
taking these as entries into passages for close
analysis. In the hands of sensitive, experienced
teachers, who give plentiful guidance, frequent re-
inforcement of what has been observed and a variety

of examples which increase pupils' confidence, many
of the available course books can be extremely helpful. In the hands of inexperienced pupils they are
likely to increase fears and confusion and so lead
to the counting and labelling which examiners
deplore.

This book is centrally concerned about pupils'
early experiences in the sixth form, about their
move from Ordinary level and CSE to the Advanced
level course. It suggests that their confidence and
enjoyment might be increased by teachers extending,
occasionally, into the sixth form those strategies
which successfully engaged younger pupils with
imaginative literature: small group discussion;
dramatised readings; personal writing. In the earlier
sections it was proposed that teachers also try to
stimulate pupils' interest in poems and prose passages by eliciting their thoughts and feelings before
class discussion and by relating these to the main
concerns of the chosen writers.

How can we draw upon the experience and knowledge which pupils already possess? How, equally
importantly, can we provide explanations, information and guidelines which will prepare pupils to
approach unfamiliar literature with some confidence?
Our main aim is to help pupils perform satisfactor-
ily in the critical examination. If we employ a
variety of strategies - those which encourage
individual response and those which introduce pupils
to a minimum of critical terminology - we might be
successful in achieving this. In spite of the inconsistencies and confusions in examination reports,
they all indicate that observant reading which takes
account of certain basic features is appreciated and
rewarded.

As far as the technical features of prose are
concerned, I suggest that teachers focus upon a
short list of simple points in their preparation and
class discussion of selected passages. In the lesson
material which follows I shall sequence and phrase
teachers' questions to introduce these points:
the topic, or content,
that is, a time of life or an experience, the
description of a person or a relationship;
the viewpoint, that is, the
author/narrator/speaker who gives information to the
reader in/outside the text;
the organisation, that is,
the order in which information is given, movements
in time, shifts in location, changes in attitude;
the types of sentences,

that is, whether they are long or short, complicated or simple, questions or statements;
the vocabulary of the
passage, whether simple or polysyllabic, concrete or
abstract, formal or colloquial;
the figures of speech, such
as personification, simile and metaphor;
the striking contrasts,
repetitions or lists.

It is possible that pupils' confidence about
recognising and commenting upon how these features
are related to the meaning of the passage will be
increased if they can first be invited to explore
material which they already know. Teachers might
begin this work by choosing passages from familiar
prose - The Lord of the Flies, The Human Element, -
say, for pupils to jot down their comments on the
central topic, the writer's viewpoint, his organisation of the material. Perhaps pupils could be given
copies of some of their own most successful writing
in order to identify these features. If they can
recognise how familiar writers and they, as writers,
have chosen and arranged language, they might
approach new material with greater confidence.

Plentiful time for pupils to consider chosen
passages is essential in the early stages of this
work. If pupils are faced with unfamiliar material
for the first time only in the lessons, their
reserve, or their anxiety to find something to say,
can produce situations when teachers deliver mini-
lectures which inhibit pupils' future confidence in
their own readings of material. Ideally, time should
be found in an earlier period for passages to be
distributed, with brief introductions and explanations, and a few questions to be considered for
pupils' contributions to a later session - the
central topic, the viewpoint, the organisation.

Many teachers who are prepared to consider the
nature and length of the introductions they or their
pupils provide for poems, appear to think these are
unnecessary for prose. We have found that, if prose
appreciation is approached through topics, in its
early stages, introductions can be usefully supportive. If, for example, the topic is childhood, it
is possible to involve pupils, before reading begins,
by inviting their own recollections and enquiring
about ways in which these might be effectively communicated. As with the poems, light mapping of prose
passages helps to introduce pupils to writers'
organisation of their material - 'firstly, we are
told', 'secondly', and so forth; 'notice where and

how the scene/time/attitude changes and whether
there are noticeable differences in the choice and
arrangement of language'.

Prose, too, needs to be prepared for its readability. Especially in the early weeks of the sixth
form it is important to find ways of avoiding unnecessary confusion or self-consciousness. It is
counterproductive to over value 'personal response'
if this means bewildering beginners or discouraging
them by public correction of their attempts to offer
interpretations of difficult, unfamiliar material.
There seems little harm in giving selected information about a writer or his background, or help with
words which have changed their meanings, together
with brief outlines of how passages are arranged,
before asking pupils to look closely at the passages
by themselves.

All this is meant to help pupils to become
familiar, gradually, with simple technical points
about how passages are written. We need to offer
quite different opportunities too, as part of our
approach to prose, for pupils to work by themselves,
to offer discoveries and interpretations without
their teachers' intervention. As was proposed in the
earlier sections, teachers might transfer their
authority to worksheets and specific, directed
questions for pupils to consider on their own or in
pairs and small groups.

With or without specific directions, pairs or
small groups can prepare public readings of all these
passages. They all demand answers to questions about
who is speaking, what the speakers are like, what
mood they are in, what their attitude is towards the
information they are giving. They all, therefore,
demand close attention to shifts in time, place and
mood and to the available clues in the author's
arrangement of language about intention and motivation. Prose, as I pointed out earlier, may provide
the best starting point for preparing public readings.

For some pupils, prose might also be the best
starting point for their own writing. More familiar
and accessible and, thus, more encouraging as
stimuli, prose passages might provide the opportunity for some pupils to show the quality of their
understanding in compositions and letters, and off
stage scenes which relate to the characters they
have discussed.

The first four passages are all about childhood.
They are on the same subject in order to increase
pupils' confidence about recognising subject matter,
viewpoint and organisation. Some pupils, we have

observed, become confused if they are introduced too rapidly to examples of prose on different subjects. They might find it helpful to remain with the same subject matter, or content, for a number of sessions and to consider several passages in which writers share similar relationships with their topic and their readers.

This particular subject matter offers other advantages. Childhood, and what we can remember about it, can be explored with all pupils - what is important, who is important, the scale of one's world, the impressions made by people and places. Pupils can also be asked to consider the possibilities available to writers who wish to re-create earlier experiences - the child's or the adult's viewpoint. It is likely, moreover, that many pupils will have been asked, at some point, to write about their own past experiences - there may even be pieces of their own writing for everyone to look at; and there is plenty of relevant material in anthologies which can be introduced as entry points or as extensions into further discussion.

What follows is a group of teacher directed lessons on passages about childhood. They consist of sequences of teacher's questions arranged to raise pupils' awareness of several simple technical features. Some teachers may decide to conduct all four sessions themselves and, later, offer pupils opportunities to work on their own on different pieces. Others may introduce matters of content, viewpoint, organisation and striking language in the first one or two and then distribute copies of the others for small group preparation. If teachers can achieve a good balance between telling and asking, between teacher directed and pupil directed activities, pupils might gradually take their teachers' key questions into their own discussions and commentaries.

## EXTRACT 1

Once upon a time and a very good time it was there was a moocow coming down along the road and this moocow that was down along the road met a nicens little boy named baby tuckoo ....

His father told him that story: his father looked at him through a glass: he had a hairy face.

He was baby tuckoo. The moocow came down the road where Betty Byrne lived: she sold lemon platt.

*O, the wild rose blossoms*
*On the little green place ...*

He sang that song. That was his song.

*O, the green wothe botheth.*

When you wet the bed, first it is warm then it gets cold. His mother put on the oilsheet. That had the queer smell.

His mother had a nicer smell than his father. She played on the piano the sailor's hornpipe for him to dance. He danced:

*Tralala lala,*
*Tralala tralaladdy,*
*Tralala lala,*
*Tralala lala.*

Uncle Charles and Dante clapped. They were older than his father and mother but Uncle Charles was older than Dante.

Dante had two brushes in her press. The brush with the maroon velvet back was for Michael Davitt and the brush with the green velvet back was for Parnell. Dante gave him a cachou every time he brought her a piece of tissue paper.

The Vances lived in number seven. They had a different father and mother. They were Eileen's father and mother. When they were grown up he was going to marry Eileen. He hid under the table. His mother said:

– O, Stephen will apologise.

Dante said:

– O, if not, the eagles will come and pull out his eyes –

Pull out his eyes,
Apologise,
Apologise,
Pull out his eyes.

Apologise,
Pull out his eyes,
Pull out his eyes,
Apologise.

James Joyce, <u>A Portrait of the Artist as a Young Man.</u>

## INTRODUCTION

The simplest and most obvious introduction to a
teacher directed class discussion of this passage is
to elicit pupils' memories of early childhood. Pupils
might be asked to jot down, as a preparation for
exchanging orally, their earliest recollections.
Teachers might ask them to think particularly about
the setting and people they can recall since these
feature in every extract. As much as half a period
might be spent on childhood memories, if teachers
intend to explore all four extracts. Pupils can be
encouraged to consider and distinguish between the
different stages of childhood - from babyhood to
adolescence, from family, home, garden and neighbourhood to school and surrounding environments. Teachers
might ask pupils to focus upon sense impressions and
to be prepared to describe their strongest associations of home, garden, neighbourhood and school. And
since these extracts introduce questions of how we
begin to make sense of our worlds - where there is
order in disorder - and the difference between
direct experience and the sequence imposed upon this
by memory - teachers might try to find ways of anticipating these during the preliminary discussion.
Before the first public reading it is worth giving
brief background information about Michael Davitt and
Parnell and explaining 'lemon platt' and 'cachou'.

## TEACHER'S QUESTIONS

### Content

Firstly, ask pupils to discover the child's name and
his likely age from close reading of all the available information: Stephen is too young to be able to
read or to pronounce all the words of the song properly; he is still called 'baby'; is still wetting
the bed; he is small enough to hide under the
table. Next, ask them to identify the other people
in the passage and to suggest how they relate
to this very young child: father, mother, auntie
and uncle, childhood playmates; public figures.
Relatives look after him and tell him stories,
tease and amuse him; children live near but in
only vaguely understood places; public figures
are introduced through everyday household objects
but have no further significance for the child.
This very elementary search for information can
be a useful, confidence building exercise which

gives pupils experience of establishing the 'subject matter', 'content' or 'theme' of the passage.

## Viewpoint

Who, pupils can be asked, is telling the story? James
Joyce is, obviously, the author, the baby's name is
Stephen and he is the 'he' referred to throughout the
passage. What, therefore, is the author doing, if he
is not writing as we might expect as an adult writer?
It is worth spending a few moments on this in order
to give pupils the opportunity of recognising the
possibility of authors' adoption of other points of
view. Most pupils can cope with this example of an
adult writer who is re-creating the world of a very
young child as if the child were speaking about
himself. Sometimes pupils raise the question of how
we see ourselves when very young - as I or he - when
most of the time we hear ourselves talked about
rather than addressed directly, and suggest that this
is why it is 'he' rather than 'I' in this extract.

## Organisation

Having established, from the age of the child, the
familiar nightly experiences, the surroundings and
the people, that this is a re-creation of bedtime
rituals from the child's point of view, pupils can
now be asked to reread the passage and jot down how
the experiences have been organised, the order in
which things happen: a fairy story at bedtime;
physical impression of father, the story teller; a
bedtime song; physical impression of mother, the
pianist; loving aunt and uncle; a reproof; a refrain.
This should enable them to attempt brief summaries
of the subject matter of the passage - childhood
experience of home and family - and to give some
answers to questions about Joyce's choice and
arrangement of language.

## Vocabulary

What explains the writer's use of simple vocabulary?
How does the child familiarise himself with new words
which are more difficult than 'glass', 'bed' and
'brushes'? How does Joyce suggest similarities between
the young child's language and the language of the
stories and rhymes? After several readings pupils

will have noticed how 'time', 'road' and 'moocow'
are repeated and also how members of his family, as
well as certain activities and objects, return inside
the child's simple statements. Next, ask pupils to
look closely at the sentences which follow the opening 'Once upon a time ...' to discover how they are
typically constructed (subject, verb, object) and to
explain why an adult writer constructs them in this
fashion. How does this relate to the subject, its
organisation and most of its vocabulary? What, un-
usually, is Joyce trying to make his language
succeed in doing for his central character?

Once the group has established that this is an
attempt to record a child's daily experiences of
bedtime within the close family, from the child's
point of view, it is valuable for them to hear the
passage reread. It is likely that, after their confidence has grown through increased familiarity,
pupils will recognise how sounds link the child's
apparently disconnected experiences. They will hear,
and gradually recognise the reason for, the repetition in 'road', 'rose', 'wothe botheth' and
'cold'. Similarly they might notice how cold relates
to the bedtime story and to the boy's recollections
of his cold, damp bed; and how smell links mother
and the child's dancing, the sounds of which relate
to Dante, the Vances and, finally, to a minor reproof
which introduces the 'apologise' refrain.

## EXTRACT 2

You don't know about me, without you have read a book by the name of "The Adventures of Tom Sawyer", but that ain't no matter....

The Widow Douglas, she took me for her son, and allowed she would sivilize me; but it was rough living in the house all the time, considering how dismal regular and decent the widow was in all her ways; and so when I couldn't stand it no longer, I lit out. I got into my old rags, and my sugar-hogshead again, and was free and satisfied. But Tom Sawyer, he hunted me up and said he was going to start a band of robbers, and I might join if I would go back to the widow and be respectable. So I went back.

The widow she cried over me, and called me a poor lost lamb, and she called me a lot of other names, too, but she never meant no harm by it. She put me in them new clothes again, and I couldn't do nothing but sweat and sweat, and feel all cramped up. Well, then, the old thing commenced again. The widow rung a bell for supper, and you had to come to time. When you got to the table you couldn't go right to eating, but you had to wait for the widow to tuck down her head and grumble a little over the victuals, though there warn't really anything the matter with them. That is, nothing only everything was cooked by itself. In a barrel of odds and ends it is different; things get mixed up, and the juice kind of swaps around, and the things go better.

After supper she got out her book and learned me about Moses and the Bulrushers; and I was in a sweat to find out all about him; but by-and-by she let it out that Moses had been dead a considerable long time; so then I didn't care no more about him; because I don't take no stock in dead people.

Pretty soon I wanted to smoke, and asked the widow to let me. But she wouldn't. She said it was a mean practice and wasn't clean, and I must try to not do it any more. That is just the way with some people. They get down on a thing when they don't know nothing about it. Here she was a-bothering about Moses, which was no kin to her, and no use to anybody, being gone, you see, yet finding a power of fault with me for doing a thing that had some good in it. And she took snuff too; of course that was all right, because she done it herself.

Her sister, Miss Watson, a tolerable slim old maid, with goggles on, had just come to live with her, and took a set at me now, with a spelling-book. She worked me middling hard for about an hour, and then the widow made her ease up. I couldn't stood it much longer. Then for an hour it was deadly dull, and I was fidgety. Miss Watson would say, "Don't put your feet up there, Huckleberry"; and "don't scrunch up like that, Huckleberry - set up straight"; and pretty soon she would say, "Don't gap and stretch like that, Huckleberry - why don't you try to behave?" Then she told me all about the bad place, and I said I wished I was there. She got mad, then, but I didn't mean no harm. All I wanted was to go somewheres; all I wanted was a change, I warn't particular. She said it was wicked to say what I said; said she wouldn't say it for the whole world;

*she* was going to live so as to go to the good place. Well, I couldn't see no advantage in going where she was going, so I made up my mind I wouldn't try for it. But I never said so, because it would only make trouble, and wouldn't do no good.

Now she had got a start, and she went on and told me all about the good place. She said all a body would have to do there was to go around all day long with a harp and sing, for ever and ever. So I didn't think much of it. But I never said so. I asked her if she reckoned Tom Sawyer would go there, and, she said, not by a considerable sight. I was glad about that, because I wanted him and me to be together.

Miss Watson she kept pecking at me, and it got tiresome and lonesome.

Mark Twain, <u>The Adventures of Huckleberry Finn</u>

There is, of course, no 'right' order in which
to approach these extracts. Teachers might choose
to begin close reading of prose with this passage
together, perhaps, with the opening of The Catcher
in the Rye, instead of the piece from James Joyce.
They might wish to start with prose in which characters address readers directly instead of moving
through re-creations of the different stages of
childhood and adolescence. The point of selecting
this extract is to give pupils the opportunity
to notice how Mark Twain chooses and arranges
language to create the impression that Huck is
speaking directly to us and sharing with us his
feelings about his evenings with the Widow and
Miss Watson. Teachers will decide, according to
their judgement of their group's confidence, whether
to read the passage aloud themselves and direct
the lesson through class questions or to ask pairs
or small groups to discuss its content, organisation
and viewpoint as preparation for giving public
readings.


INTRODUCTION

After a brief introduction to the book and explaining, if necessary, 'Tom Sawyer', 'Moses', 'sugar
hogshead' and 'victuals', read the passage aloud.
Ask pupils to begin forming impressions of the
speaker and his life with Widow Douglas and Miss
Watson. Perhaps map the extract lightly by referring
to movements in place and time.


TEACHER'S QUESTIONS

Content

Ask pupils to reread the passage, alone or in
pairs, looking for all the factual information
it contains about the three characters. Ask them,
first, to find out Huck's likely age and situation
as well as what we learn about his background
and customary way of life. Then ask them to look
equally closely at what we are told about the
Widow and her sisters - their good intentions
(took him 'for her son', cried over him, gave
him 'new clothes again', regular food, religious
instruction and basic education) and their strict-
ness about grace, Bible reading, smoking and Huck's
restlessness.

123

## Organisation

Once it has been agreed that this is an adolescent
boy's account of his unwilling submission to two
middle aged women's domestic routine, ask pupils
to look at where the passage is set, how it moves
in time and the different kind of information
it includes. If pupils observe how first the narrative moves quickly inside and outside the Widow's
home and then remains inside for the length of
an unbearably tedious evening for Huck, they may
realise how these shifts suggest his restlessness
and sense of the slow passing of time. We have
already seen how James Joyce shaped Stephen's
early experience of his environment by recording
the child's main sense impressions. Here Twain
takes us inside and outside the Widow's home and
then remains inside for the rest of the time to
convey Huck's indecisiveness and the penalty he
pays for being 'sivilized'. The passage opens
with the boy's determination to leave and closes
with his feeling of loneliness on having been
taken in as 'her son'.

## Viewpoint

This can be considered in two ways, by looking
at the direct address, the simple vocabulary and
sentence structure and then by looking at Huck's
attitude towards his experiences. Pupils quickly
appreciate that Mark Twain has removed himself, as
author, and speaks to us through his central characters - 'You don't know about me'. They were encouraged to notice the simple vocabulary and sentences in the first passage and to relate these
features to early childhood. Here they can be asked
to be similarly observant about how Mark Twain has
tried to make Huck sound like an uneducated adolescent - the misspellings and mispronunciations; the
simple, slangy vocabulary: 'I lit out'; 'juice kind
of swaps around'; 'I don't take no stock in dead
people'; 'I warn't particular'; 'she kept pecking
at me'. Sentences are either short - 'So I didn't
think much of it' - or long but made up of
information linked by 'and' and 'but'. Huck's story
telling, with its 'then', 'now', 'after' and 'soon',
his inclusion of bits of conversation during the
evening, both contribute to our strong impression
of his own speaking voice.
   Teachers who want pupils to consider viewpoint
in closer detail will ask them to look at Huck's

attitude towards his readers and at his feelings
about the experience of being civilised. Firstly
ask them to notice what he confides in us and
keeps secret from the two women. What is the effect
of being told, for example, that 'I couldn't do
nothing but sweat and sweat and feel all cramped
up' and 'I was glad about that because I wanted
him and me to be together'? Secondly ask pupils
to consider Huck's conflicting feelings about
the Widow and her sister. He partly respects them
– 'regular and decent'; 'cried over me and called
me a poor lost lamb'; 'learned me about Moses and
the Bulrushers'. He partly resents and criticises
them – 'dismal regular'; 'they get down on a thing
when they don't know nothing about it'; 'she kept
pecking at me'. Some pupils quickly realise that
Mark Twain is encouraging experienced adult readers
to be more critical of the women's inflexibility
than Huck is capable of being at this point. For
many, though, it might be helpful, at this stage,
to limit observations simply to the content and
organisation of the extract and to the author's
choice of a direct address to his readers by a dis-
gruntled adolescent.

   After having considered the content, organisation, viewpoint, sentences and vocabulary in extracts from Huckleberry Finn and, perhaps, The
Catcher in the Rye as well, some teachers might
choose to reinforce pupils' awareness of these
points by asking them to attempt similar writing
of their own. Efforts to re-create particular periods
of their own lives, placing these precisely and
adopting a personal, confidential relationship
with a reader, might strengthen pupils' observation
of some features of imaginative literature. It
might be especially valuable to try this before
moving on to the following passages, in which
authors are writing as adults about their child-
hoods and inviting readers to look backwards with
them.

EXTRACT 3

The first objects that assume a distinct presence before me, as I look far back, into the blank of my infancy, are my mother with her pretty hair and youthful shape, and Peggotty, with no shape at all, and eyes so dark that they seemed to darken their whole neighbourhood in her face, and cheeks and arms so hard and red that I wondered the birds didn't peck her in preference to apples.

I believe I can remember these two at a little distance apart, dwarfed to my sight by stooping down or kneeling on the floor, and I going unsteadily from the one to the other. I have an impression of my mind which I cannot distinguish from actual remembrance, of the touch of Peggotty's forefinger as she used to hold it out to me, and of its being roughened by needlework, like a pocket nutmeg-grater ...

... There comes out of the cloud, our house - not new to me, but quite familiar, in its earliest remembrance. On the ground-floor is Peggotty's kitchen opening into a back yard; with a pigeon-house on a pole, in the centre, without any pigeons in it; a great dog-kennel in a corner, without any dog; and a quantity of fowls that look terribly tall to me, walking about in a menacing and ferocious manner. There is one cock who gets upon a post to crow, and seems to take particular notice of me as I look at him through the kitchen window, who makes me shiver, he is so fierce. Of the geese outside the side-gate who came waddling after me with their long necks stretched out when I go that way, I dream at night; as a man environed by wild beasts might dream of lions.

Charles Dickens, <u>David Copperfield</u>

Approaches to Prose

The next two passages are included for the opportunities they offer to strengthen pupils' confidence about how to read prose extracts closely and to comment upon a selection of features: content, viewpoint, organisation, sentence structure, figurative language and vocabulary. They, too, are attempts by imaginative writers to communicate the experiences of early childhood and they relate well to the earlier passages because they also include family figures and familiar places. The obvious difference is their viewpoint and it is partly for pupils to be observant about this that the extracts have been chosen.


TEACHER'S QUESTIONS

Viewpoint

Since Dickens' subject matter is made explicit - infancy, 'going unsteadily from one to another', the fowls which seemed 'terribly tall' - ask pupils, when they have heard this passage read aloud, firstly to find statements which tell us about the author's standpoint. Finding these provides a starting point from which to recognise that here the subject is more the effort of remembering than the actual experience of being a child. It is useful for pupils to look through the passage to discover how many times Dickens expresses his attempts to remember: 'as I look far back'; 'I believe I can remember'; 'I have an impression in my mind'; 'there comes out of the cloud'.


Organisation; vocabulary

Next, perhaps, after spending a few moments recalling how Stephen's impressions were presented in A Portrait of the Artist, ask pupils to look at how information is organised here. How is Dickens' organisation different from James Joyce's? Perhaps pupils might realise that when the author is in obvious control we are kept at a greater distance from the child's experiences. Recalling, too, their own efforts to remember childhood, pupils might appreciate the difference between being inside and outside the child's or adolescent's mind. Ask pupils to choose the points in this passage where the experiences are especially childlike and to be prepared to relate these to how they are written:

'birds', 'apples', 'Peggotty's forefinger', 'pocket
nutmeg-grater', 'pigeon house on a pole', 'great
dog kennel', 'fowls', 'cock on a post'.

Next ask them what is also present in the descriptions which confirms our impression of the adult
writer's viewpoint. Which words and phrases are un-
childlike? 'A distinct presence'; 'I cannot distinguish from actual rememberance';   'a menacing
and ferocious manner'; 'as a man environed by
wild beasts might dream of lions'.

## Sentences

Finally it might be useful, especially if pupils
have explored the first two passages, for them to
hear, or reread this extract in order to notice how
the sentences here are differently structured. After
having looked closely at the extracts from Joyce and
Twain,   pupils are likely to notice upon close in-
spection of this passage - without needing to employ
grammatical terms - that, except for one, all the
sentences are long and complex. In the first term of
the lower sixth, and probably in the Advanced level
examination too, it is sufficient for pupils to
notice this and to relate their observation to the
author who is writing, as himself, about childhood.
Some pupils might volunteer that the greater complexity of these sentences relate to what, precisely,
is different about the passage, that it is partly
about the effort of memory. It would be interesting
to discover whether pupils could identify this and
relate the differences in 'style' (between the two
passages) to the contrasting nature of the attempts
being made to 'look far back'.

## EXTRACT 4

Radiating from that house, with its crumbling walls, its thumps and shadows, its fancied foxes under the floor, I moved along paths that lengthened inch by inch with my mounting strength of days. From stone to stone in the trackless yard I sent forth my acorn shell of senses, moving through unfathomable oceans like a South Sea savage island-hopping across the Pacific. Antennae of eyes and nose and grubbing fingers captured a new tuft of grass, a fern, a slug, the skull of a bird, a grotto of bright snails. Through the long summer ages of those first few days I enlarged my world and mapped in my mind its secure havens, its dust-deserts and puddles, its peaks of dirt and flag-flying bushes. Returning too, dry-throated, over and over again, to its several well-prodded horrors: the bird's gaping bones in its cage of old sticks; the black flies in the corner, slimy dead; dry rags of snakes; and the crowded, rotting silent-roaring city of a cat's grub-captured carcass.

Once seen, these relics passed within the frontiers of the known lands, to be remembered with a buzzing in the ears, to be revisited when the stomach was strong. They were the first tangible victims of that destroying force whose job I knew went on both night and day, though I could never catch him at it. Nevertheless I was grateful for them. Though they haunted my eyes and stuck in my dreams, they reduced for me the first infinite possibilities of horror. They chastened the imagination with the proof of a limited frightfulness.

From the harbour mouth of the scullery door I learned the rocks and reefs and the channels where safety lay. I discovered the physical pyramid of the cottage, its stores and labyrinths, its centres of magic, and of the green, sprouting island-garden upon which it stood. My Mother and sisters sailed past me like galleons in their busy dresses, and I learned the smells and sounds which followed in their wakes, the surge of breath, air of carbolic, song and grumble, and smashing of crockery.

Laurie Lee, <u>Cider With Rosie</u>

This extract from <u>Cider with Rosie</u> can be looked at in isolation, of course, or considered in sequence with the previous extract in order to reinforce some of the points raised in the discussion of <u>David Copperfield</u>.

## INTRODUCTION

Ask pupils to recall both the childlike elements and the evidence of an adult perspective which they encountered in the David Copperfield extract, that is, recall the setting, people, scale of objects, and the evidence within the passage of the author making an effort to remember his past. Introduce this extract as having much in common with the earlier one, even though it belongs to the twentieth century. Tell pupils that they will be asked to notice the precise period of childhood which Laurie Lee is describing and to explain how his choice and arrangement of language relate to the topic which concerns him. Point out that it is similar to the David Copperfield passage in that it includes the view of the adult writer looking back upon himself. Some pupils will have read <u>Cider with Rosie</u> earlier in the school and can be invited to recall the times, places, family figures and key episodes as part of an introduction to the passage. Perhaps they can comment upon how Laurie Lee set about communicating childhood experiences and how he, as adult writer, featured in his book. Read the passage aloud and then give pupils an opportunity to reread it by themselves.

## Content

In pairs or small groups pupils can discuss the passage and jot down what each section is about and try to prepare brief statements about each paragraph: the child's exploration of the garden; the adult's comments upon his early experiences; the child's discovery of the rest of the cottage in the safe company of his family. These jottings can either be exchanged for partner's or other pair's comments, or contributed to class discussion. Once content and overall organisation have been agreed, pupils can be asked to give evidence from the passage about the particular stage of this child's life, looking carefully at where he is and how he moves: paths, stones, tufts of grass, puddles, various insects and dead animals; 'inch by inch', 'stone by stone', 'scullery door'.

They might be asked, too, about other ways in which Laurie Lee suggests inexperience, someone at the very beginning of life. Discussion of 'acorn of senses' and 'South Sea savage island-hopping' might prepare for a later stage of the lesson which focuses upon the effects of the travelling and voyaging figures of speech.

## Point of View

Like Dickens, Laurie Lee is writing from his adult standpoint about his past. Though this passage is full of childhood's movements and experiences, the author is present throughout as himself. Ask pupils to look for evidence of this. Firstly there is the obvious difference between this and James Joyce's and Salinger's direct address from the child's and adolescent's viewpoint. Here the writer is telling us what the child was doing and includes his judgement of its significance: 'I moved', 'I sent forth', 'I enlarged my world', 'I learned ...' Secondly there is his adult commentary in the second paragraph.

## Vocabulary

Ask pupils to collect examples of where the vocabulary is at its simplest: 'house', 'walls', 'thumps', 'foxes', right through to 'song and grumble' and 'smashing of crockery'. They might, if they can keep their copies of the passage, identify these simple words by underlining them in coloured pencils. After sharing opinions about their collections, ask them to do the same thing with words which are characteristic of the adult author: 'radiating', 'unfathomable', 'antennae', 'havens', through to 'labyrinths'.

Noticeably, the most complex vocabulary is in the middle paragraph. Although, as in the Dickens passage the vocabulary is mixed throughout, there is a section of this one which shows clearly where its complexity is related to Lee's adult commentary, his adult interest in the effects of certain experiences upon his childhood self: 'They were the first tangible victims'; '... they reduced for me the first infinite possibilities ...'; 'They chastened the imagination ...'

## Figures of Speech

Teachers who are keen to offer their pupils opportunities for expressing approval and disapproval of
writers' descriptions might like to ask them to
explore the travelling and voyaging imagery in this
passage. The acorn metaphor, alongside the savage
South Sea islander has already been included and
related to the early stages of growth and primitive
understanding.

Some pupils might find it helpful to be given a
few moments to explore the passage by themselves to
note or underline 'the trackless yard', 'unfathomable
oceans', 'island hopping', right through to 'island-
garden' and 'galleons' to have an opportunity to see,
as well as hear, the extended travelling imagery.

They then can be asked why Laurie Lee chose
these figures and to explain how they relate to the
subject of the extract. How appropriate do pupils
think these are in this passage? How appropriate is
the image of the sea? Trying to avoid imposing their
own likely dissatisfactions with this, teachers might
invite pupils to consider ways in which this image
relates well to the central experience and how it
fails in relation to the precise physical surroundings which the child is exploring. Thus, an opportunity might be taken to elicit pupils' associations
with the images in a passage and for them to express
their views about how successfully a writer has
aroused their imaginations through his choice of
language.

EXTRACT 5

The wind by now was more than redoubled. The shutters were bulging as if tired elephants were leaning against them, and Father was trying to tie the fastening with that handkerchief. But to push against this wind was like pushing against rock. The handkerchief, shutters, everything burst: the rain poured in like the sea into a sinking ship, the wind occupied the room, snatching pictures from the wall, sweeping the table bare. Through the gaping frames the lightning–lit scene without was visible. The creepers, which before had looked like cobwebs, now streamed up into the sky like new-combed hair. Bushes were lying flat, laid back on the ground as close as a rabbit lays back his ears. Branches were leaping about loose in the sky. The negro huts were clean gone, and the negroes crawling on their stomachs across the compound to gain the shelter of the house. The bouncing rain seemed to cover the ground with a white smoke, a sort of sea in which the blacks wallowed like porpoises. One nigger–boy began to roll away: his mother, forgetting caution, rose to her feet: and immediately the fat old beldam was blown clean away, bowling along across fields and hedgerows like some one in a funny fairy–story, till she fetched up against a wall and was pinned there, unable to move. But the others managed to reach the house, and soon could be heard in the cellar underneath.

Richard Hughes, <u>A High Wind in Jamaica</u>

I have chosen the next two extracts as examples of lesson material because of the contrast in viewpoints they offer on similar subjects. Richard Hughes' description, which presents the storm through a child's eyes, is written in noticeably simple sentences and vocabulary; Conrad's description, through a sailor's eyes, is, at times, very complex. Teachers will choose either to ask pupils, individually or in groups, to work on these descriptions and to prepare responses for class discussion, or to conduct discussion on one or both themselves.

Thus far, we have been concentrating on a single topic - author's re-creations of particular stages of childhood and youth. Pupils may be growing confident about their ability to discover from the given information in extracts, and from features of writer's language, whether they are written from the child's or adult's viewpoint. After hearing and then re-reading the selected passage from A High Wind in Jamaica we hope that pupils will recognise that Hughes is writing about a dramatic event in a child's life and re-creating this as it might have appeared to the child.


INTRODUCTION

This might consist of a light mapping of the passage to anticipate its shift of focus from the inside to the outside of the house. It might be simply a request that pupils try to be observant about the kind of weather which is being described and where it is likely to be happening.


CLASS DISCUSSION

Content

After pupils have heard the passage read aloud, ask them to reread it privately and to jot down brief notes about this storm and its likely setting. From the information we are given about the storm's ferocity - 'shutters were bulging', 'everything burst', 'the rain poured in', 'the wind occupied the room' - and from the references to 'negro huts' and 'nigger boy', we know that this is tropical weather. A hurricane is disrupting normal home life. By looking for answers to very basic questions about what is actually happening in their extracts pupils are gaining experience in summarising content, or subject matter. It might be useful, occasionally, for everyone to attempt a summary of an extract and for versions to be compared, discussed and modified.

## Viewpoint

Next, ask pupils to discover, from all the available information, who is giving the account of this event, and where the speaker is whilst the hurricane is attacking the house. It should be clear from 'Father was trying ...' and 'Through the gaping frames ...' that the child is recording her impressions from her position near the broken shutters.

Having established this, pupils might continue to produce more evidence of the author's attempt to describe this scene from Emily's viewpoint.

## Vocabulary

Reminding them that we know this scene is being described by a child, ask pupils to find whatever they think, apart from the reference to 'father', conveys this viewpoint in the extract. What, that is, is especially childlike about it - perhaps, 'like someone in a funny fairy story', 'tired elephants', 'like new combed hair', 'as close as a rabbit lays his ears'? Perhaps the mainly simple and concrete vocabulary - wind, shutters, handkerchief, rain, wind, table, frames, creepers.

## Organisation

Next it is useful to ask pupils to reread this passage, noticing where each part takes place and what, precisely, is being concentrated upon. They quickly notice that Hughes firstly describes the inside of the house - shutters, pictures, table.

Once the shutters have burst, the scene changes - where? 'The lightning-lit scene without'. After the changed location has been established, ask what the writer next describes - creepers, bushes, branches, that is, the outside landscape. Finally, people are swept into view - negroes crawling on their stomachs; one nigger boy, his mother, the others managed to reach ...

## Sentences

Gradually pupils may come to recognise how this passage is organised - inside, outside; nature, people; above (shutters) to below (in the cellar underneath). And having commented upon this they can be asked to consider the sentences within each section, bearing in mind both the topic - the violent storm - and the child's viewpoint. They can simply look at the length of the sentences. How might their varying lengths be related to what is being described? Those describing the wind, the lightning, the leaping branches - all swift movements - are very short, to communicate the speed of these natural actions. The sentences describing the family's efforts to preserve the shutters, the rain pouring in, the negroes crawling, the blowing over of the negro woman and her son are noticeably longer. Once pupils have become familiar with this passage and have had opportunities to comment upon the different parts of the scene it describes, they might be asked to look, too, at the structure of each of the sentences. They might be asked to suggest why almost every sentence begins with its subject: the wind, the shutters, the handkerchief, the creepers, the bushes. It is likely that, at this stage, pupils will suggest how this arrangement contributes towards the overall effect of frightening and destructive energy.

After several readings, each focusing upon specific features - subject, viewpoint, organisation, choice and arrangement of language, it is hoped that pupils will have recognised and can comment confidently upon the following:

> the ferocity of the tropical storm;
> the child in the house at the gaping window;
> the shifts of location within the scene;
> how the lengths and construction of sentences relate to the activities in the passage;
> the relationship between the narrator and the figures of speech and vocabulary.

Some teachers might ask pupils to prepare a draft of a commentary on the passage from their jottings and, for homework, to redraft a finished version. Others might ask them to attempt a piece of writing about the effects of severe weather, which re-creates a scene at a precise place and time from a chosen point of view.

EXTRACT 6

Sails blew adrift. Things broke loose. Cold and wet, we were washed about the deck while trying to repair damages. The ship tossed about, shaken furiously, like a toy in the hand of a lunatic. Just at sunset there was a rush to shorten sail before the menace of a sombre hail cloud. The hard gust of wind came brutal like the blow of a fist. The ship relieved of her canvas in time received it pluckily: she yielded reluctantly to the violent onset; then, coming up with a stately and irresistible motion, brought her spars to windward in the teeth of the screeching squall. Out of the abysmal darkness of the black cloud overhead white hail streamed on her, rattled on the rigging, leaped in handfuls off the yards, rebounded on the deck - round and gleaming in the murky turmoil like a shower of pearls. It passed away. For a moment a livid sun shot horizontally the last rays of sinister light between the hills of steep, rolling waves. Then a wild night rushed in - stamped out in a great howl that dismal remnant of a stormy day.

There was no sleep on board that night. Most seamen remembered in their life one or two such nights of a culminating gale. Nothing seems left of the whole universe but darkness, clamour, fury - and the ship. And like the last vestige of a shattered creation she drifts, bearing an anguished remnant of sinful mankind, through the distress, tumult, and pain of an avenging terror. No one slept in the forecastle. The tin oil-lamp suspended on a long string, smoking, described wide circles; wet clothing made dark heaps on the glistening floor; a thin layer of water rushed to and fro. In the bed-places men lay booted, resting on elbows and with open eyes. Hung-up suits of oil-skin swung out and in, lively and disquieting like reckless ghosts of decapitated seamen dancing in a tempest. No one spoke and all listened. Outside the night moaned and sobbed to the accompaniment of a continuous loud tremor as of innumerable drums beating far off. Shrieks passed through the air. Tremendous dull blows made the ship tremble while she rolled under the weight of the seas toppling on her deck. At times she soared up swiftly as if to leave this earth for ever, then during interminable moments fell through a void with all the hearts on board of her standing still, till a frightful shock, expected and sudden, started them off again with a big thump ... Now and then, for the fraction of an intolerable second, the ship, in the fiercer burst of a terrible uproar, remained on her side, vibrating and still, with a stillness more appalling than the wildest motion. Then upon all those prone bodies a stir would pass, a shiver of suspense. A man would protrude his anxious head and a pair of eyes glistened in the sway of light glaring wildly. Some moved their legs a little as if making ready to jump out. But several, motionless on their backs and with one hand gripping hard the edge of the bunk, smoked nervously with quick puffs, staring upwards; immobilized in a great craving for peace.

Joseph Conrad, The Nigger of the 'Narcissus'

## INTRODUCTION

This passage also describes a ferocious storm,
a gale at sea which persists throughout the night.
After this brief introduction, ask pupils to follow
a public reading. They might then be given the
complete period to reread, discuss the passage
among themselves and prepare notes on what is
happening at each stage, what the experience is
like for the crew and how this is communicated.
Pupils could be asked to prepare public readings
which convey the changing moods in the passage.
A teacher directed lesson, however, might take
the following pattern.

## CLASS DISCUSSION

### Viewpoint

Having been told that this is about a gale at
sea and listened to the passage read aloud, pupils
might explore this description to discover who the
narrator is. We hope that they will notice that he
is present from the opening when, 'cold and wet, we
were washed about the deck while trying to repair
the damages'. We hope that they will discover his
involvement from his description of happenings on
board in technical terms - 'canvas', 'spars to
windward', 'rigging', 'forecastle'. He is, therefore, author/sailor, telling readers about events
and responses whilst sharing the crew's experiences.

### Organisation

By now pupils are becoming familiar with movements
within descriptions - in place and time and between
people and moods. Ask them, therefore, to spend a
few moments tracing, firstly, the movement in this
passage about the ship. Discovering, and perhaps
underlining or jotting notes on, the different
locations - deck, forecastle, the bed-places, the
bunk - might help to strengthen their awareness of
the overall movement within this description from
the storm to the tensions among the crew.
　　Ask them, then, to note (using underlining
pencils or scrap paper) the movements in time -
'at sunset', 'a wild night rushed in', 'that night'.
Which parts are the longest and most detailed?
　　Next give pupils a little time to read through
this passage looking at the sailors' actions to see

the changes here. What are they doing at each stage and what is the main difference between the beginning and ending?

Pupils who respond observantly to an opening request to notice how this description moves in place and time might be asked to prepare comments on all the other developments and contrasts, on their own. Many are likely to be confident about this after having been asked publicly about the main shifts, and heard these shared and agreed.

What we hope is that, gradually, they will become aware of all the movements back and forth in this passage - between the gale and the ship, the outside and the inside, the noise and the silence, the ship's movements and the crew - realise that the crew's fear comes from the irregularity and caprice of the unknown.

## Sentences

Preparing to read this description aloud, and listening to prepared readings, are the best ways to experience the effects of changing sentence lengths and rhythms. Reminding pupils that this description is re-creating sailors' experiences during a severe storm, ask them to look closely at how Conrad has organised his chosen words.

Why are the opening sentences so short? Where else in the passage does he write short sentences and what is their effect? Having observed that the opening of the storm and the men's first responses are described in short sentences, move on to reread the noticeably longer ones. Have the longest read aloud by different pupils.

Explore the relationship between sentence lengths and the event described. Firstly, there is the ship's response to the 'blow of a fist' - 'received it pluckily', 'yielded reluctantly', 'coming up' ... There is also the long sentence describing the 'streams of hail' corresponding to the length of a stream and the time it takes to rebound on the deck. Additionally, there are long sentences describing the sounds of the night and, most strikingly, the ones which describe the heights and depths to which the boat soars and falls, remaining vibrating 'on her side', and those telling of the tormented discomfort of the men. It is hoped that, gradually, pupils will become aware of a pattern in the passage. The weather's behaviour is described in mainly short, simple sentences; the ship's responses and the men's discomfort are more complex and are described in correspondingly more complex structures.

## Vocabulary

This experience, it will have been agreed, is physical. Pupils can be asked, therefore, to identify vocabulary which forces readers to be aware of this, which brings them close to the writer's sensations. It is frequently technical, making us aware of the different parts of the boat, and frequently simple and concrete; sails, wet clothing, suits of oil-skin, legs, backs, bunk. Where, unlike the previous passage, is the vocabulary more complex? What are their views on the effects of this? Remembering the viewpoint of the sailor, the man of action, how might the figures of speech be considered from that perspective - 'the toy', 'the fist', 'the shower of pearls', 'the drums'? Some time might usefully be spent on asking pupils to think about each of these and to attempt explanations of each in this scene as described by this particular character.

## Further Observations

Some pupils might notice how Conrad introduces the sailors' gloom during the long dangerous night through images associated with death: suspended on a long string; dark heaps on the glistening floor; oil-skins swing in and out. If they were to be asked to look closely at the scene inside the boat during the night, some might notice the repeated negatives - 'nothing seemed left'; 'no one slept'; 'no one spoke'; 'motionless on their backs'; 'immobilised in a great craving for peace'.

We have been impressed frequently by how much pupils are prepared to volunteer about the details they have noticed in a passage when they have become comfortable and confident about the central questions of topic, viewpoint and organisation. Given time to reflect alone, or to discuss together, further effects of writers' choice and arrangement of language, they are perceptive and observant about, say, 'hills of waves' and 'tremble while she rolled under the weight of seas toppling on her deck'. In the early stages of this work they are often reluctant to express these responses until a secure framework has been established in which to talk about the topic, its organisation and most striking arrangements of language.

These final extracts are the most complex in this
section. Thus far, especially in the early extracts
about childhood, authors have either identified completely with their characters by speaking through
them, or made their sympathy evident by letting
readers know that they are describing themselves at
different stages of their lives. The two extracts
which follow, however, are descriptions of women by
detached, critical observers. Henry James' Mrs.
Farrinder is a confident, middle aged matron who
spends most of her time addressing public meetings.
Here she is described from the standpoint of a critical observer who has witnessed her performances on
and off the platform. George Eliot's Dorothea is a
rich, unmarried girl who is troubled by uncertainties
and who spends her time on a variety of contrasting
activities. She is described from several different
critical standpoints, including her own.

Viewpoint has been important, of course, in all
the literature we have considered. Authors so far,
though, have not appealed to us over their characters' heads; unlike Henry James and George Eliot,
they have not introduced readers to distinctions and
contrasts between opinions which characters hold of
themselves and those held of them by others. We hope
that pupils will have some sense, from their initial
readings, that these women are both forceful and
slightly absurd, and then go on to discover how this
impression has been created. What might first alert
them to the two characters' lack of self awareness -
Mrs. Farrinder's husband Amariah perhaps, and
Dorothea's vanity in readily conferring upon her
sister a suitor whom she despises - might direct
attention to other features of the two passages:
their organisation, the structure of their sentences,
the repetitions and contrasts.

The **description of Mrs. Farrinder is the** simpler
of the two extracts. It concentrates exclusively
upon her and the effect the narrator claims she has
upon those who attend her public meetings. Once this
has been established pupils can be encouraged to
look closely at the viewpoint in the passage, how
the speaker organises the information, the structure
of his sentences and choice of vocabulary to decide
how these affect our impressions of the central
character. Apart from a reference to her dress - she
had a rustling dress - the physical descriptions of
Mrs. Farrinder could be of a man - handsome, angularity, air of success, noble. What might we be
meant to think of this? What does this tell us about
the narrator himself? Teachers who prefer pupils to

work on their own, to discuss this passage and report back in a general discussion, might briefly raise questions of this sort. They might very usefully ask pupils to consider the tone of voice in which this description should be publicly delivered.

EXTRACT 7

She was a copious, handsome woman, in whom angularity had been corrected by the air of success; she had a rustling dress (it was evident what *she* thought about taste), abundant hair of a glossy blackness, a pair of folded arms, the expression of which seemed to say that rest, in such a career as hers, was as sweet as it was brief, and a terrible regularity of feature. I apply that adjective to her fine placid mask because she seemed to face you with a question of which the answer was preordained, to ask you how to countenance could fail to be noble of which the measurements were so correct. You could contest neither the measurements nor the nobleness, and had to feel that Mrs. Farrinder imposed herself. There was a lithographic smoothness about her, and a mixture of the American matron and the public character. There was something public in her eye, which was large, cold and quiet; it had acquired a sort of exposed reticence from the habit of looking down from a lecture-desk, over a sea of heads, while its distinguished owner was eulogised by a leading citizen. Mrs. Farrinder, at almost any time, had the air of being introduced by a few remarks. She talked with great slowness and distinctness, and evidently a high sense of responsibility; she pronounced every syllable of every word and insisted on being explicit. If, in conversation with her, you attempted to take anything for granted, or to jump two or three steps at a time, she paused, looking at you with a cold patience, as if she knew that trick, and then went on at her own measured pace. She lectured on temperance and the rights of women; the ends she laboured for were to give the ballot to every woman in the country and to take the flowing bowl from every man. She was held to have a very fine manner, and to embody the domestic virtues and the graces of the drawing-room; to be shining proof, in short, that the forum, for ladies, is not necessarily hostile to the fireside. She had a husband, and his name was Amariah.

Henry James, <u>The Bostonians</u>

Approaches to Prose

INTRODUCTION

A short preliminary class discussion about describing
public figures might introduce the first reading. It
might be helpful for pupils to spend a few moments
thinking about what information is generally available to us about public men and women - royalty,
politicians, entertainers - if we have only their
public appearances to draw upon. They are likely to
agree about appearance, manner, speech, their treatment of people who are interviewing them and being
introduced to them. A task which might anticipate
this passage would be to prepare notes of this kind
on a well known national or local figure. When these
are exchanged pupils can be encouraged to notice the
differences between their descriptions and how these
were conveyed in their language. Like the narrators
in the following extracts they will probably have
given direct descriptions of the public figure and
indirect information about themselves. Many pupils
will need explanations of unfamiliar vocabulary
before the first public reading: lithographic;
eulogised; temperance.


CLASS DISCUSSION

Content

Ask pupils to reread the passage, noting all the
available information about Mrs. Farrinder, apart
from her appearance and the impression she makes. It
is a useful exercise at this early stage to collect
the facts in the passage and to observe the order in
which they are given. We are hoping that, with
practice, pupils will feel confident enough to sum-
marise the 'subject' or 'content' of a passage: a
married middle aged female public speaker, whose
special topics are temperance and votes for women.

Organisation

Next, or at the same time as performing the first
task, pupils might note the order in which readers
are given information about Mrs. Farrinder. We hope
that they will observe that the first section of the
extract is about her physical appearance - 'copious',
'handsome', 'rustling dress', 'abundant hair', 'folded arms' ... 'cold quiet eye'. The second section, introduced by her name, is about meeting her, the impression made upon the narrator by her conversation -

'talked with great slowness'; 'pronounced every syllable'; 'went on at her own measured pace'. Finally, the narrator tells readers what people say about Mrs. Farrinder - 'held to have a very fine manner'; 'to embody domestic virtues'; 'to be a shining proof'. What, therefore, is going on and in what order? How might the shape of this description affect our view of Mrs. Farrinder?

## Viewpoint

Whether in small group discussion or through teachers' question, two points need to be considered: the apparent relationship between Mrs. Farrinder and the narrator; the narrator's opinion of the public speaker. Teachers might ask pupils to discuss these on their own and then to prepare public readings which convey the observer's view of the central character.

## Sentences

Having discussed pupils' recognition of the overall organisation of the passage and the narrator's viewpoint, not forgetting the positioning of Mrs. Farrinder's husband at the very end, ask them to look at how most of the sentences are organised. Without needing to know the terms of formal grammar, they can see that they are noticeably long and complicated. Only the sentences which describe Mrs. Farrinder's 'air' and her husband are short, and pupils can usually suggest reasons for this. Why, they can be asked to consider, might the author include so much in each sentence? In what ways do the long and short sentences differ as they relate to Mrs. Farrinder? What are we being told, in most of the sentences, in addition to simple recorded facts about the woman? It emerges, after close consideration, especially when standpoint has been noted, that the writer is telling his readers about Mrs. Farrinder and the impression she makes on someone who attends her meeting and is introduced to her after the platform speeches. The author/narrator is explaining how Mrs. Farrinder strikes him; 'it was evident what she thought about taste'; 'she seemed to face you with a question to which the answer was preordained'; 'as if she knew that trick'.

Ask, too, for close attention to each sentence for discovery of how its organisation makes Mrs. Farrinder appear aggressive and rather frightening.

In addition to being told about the 'terrible
regularity of feature' and the 'fine placid mask' we
come, perhaps, to share the observer's sense of
being under threat, from the repeated structure
which puts her at the beginning of the sentence:
she was, she had; 'Mrs. Farrinder had the air',
**'she talked'**, 'she pronounced', 'she lectured',
'she had a husband'. Sometimes words and phrases
are repeated - 'noble', 'correct', 'measurements';
'every syllable', 'every word', 'every woman',
'every man'; 'public character', 'public eye';
'fine mask', 'fine manner'. Some constructions,
too: 'the expression of which seemed to say';
'she seemed to face you'; 'she was held to have
...'.

EXTRACT 8

And how should Dorothea not marry? - a girl so handsome and with such prospects? Nothing could hinder it but her love of extremes, and her insistence on regulating life according to notions which might cause a wary man to hesitate before he made her an offer, or even might lead her at last to refuse all offers. A young lady of some birth and fortune, who knelt suddenly down on a brick floor by the side of a sick labourer and prayed fervidly as if she thought herself living in the time of the Apostles - who had strange whims of fasting like a Papist, and of sitting up at night to read old theological books! Such a wife might awaken you some fine morning with a new scheme for the application of her income which would interfere with political economy and the keeping of saddle-horses: a man would naturally think twice before he risked himself in such fellowship. Women were expected to have weak opinions; but the great safeguard of society and of domestic life was, that opinions were not acted on. Sane people did what their neighbours did, so that if any lunatics were at large, one might know and avoid them.

The rural opinion about the new young ladies, even among the cottagers, was generally in favour of Celia, as being so amiable and innocent-looking, while Miss Brooke's large eyes seemed, like her religion, too unusual and striking. Poor Dorothea! compared with her, the innocent-looking Celia was knowing and worldly-wise; so much subtler is a human mind than the outside tissues which make a sort of blazonry or clock-face for it.

Yet those who approached Dorothea, though prejudiced against her by this alarming hearsay, found that she had a charm unaccountably reconcilable with it. Most men thought her bewitching when she was on horseback. She loved the fresh air and the various aspects of the country, and when her eyes and cheeks glowed with mingled pleasure she looked very little like a devotee. Riding was an indulgence which she allowed herself in spite of conscientious qualms; she felt that she enjoyed it in a pagan sensuous way, and always looked forward to renouncing it.

She was open, ardent, and not in the least self-admiring; indeed, it was pretty to see how her imagination adorned her sister Celia with attractions altogether superior to her own, and if any gentleman appeared to come to the Grange from some other motive than that of seeing Mr Brooke, she concluded that he must be in love with Celia: Sir James Chettam, for example, whom she constantly considered from Celia's point of view, inwardly debating whether it would be good for Celia to accept him. That he should be regarded as a suitor to herself would have seemed to her a ridiculous irrelevance. Dorothea, with all her eagerness to know the truths of life, retained very childlike ideas about marriage. She felt sure that she would have accepted the judicious Hooker, if she had been born in time to save him from that wretched mistake he made in matrimony; or John Milton when his blindness had come on; or any of the other great men whose odd habits it would have been glorious piety to endure; but an amiable handsome baronet, who said 'Exactly' to her remarks even when she expressed uncertainty, - how could he affect her as a lover? The really delightful marriage must be that where your husband was a sort of father, and could teach you even Hebrew, if you wished it.

George Eliot, <u>Middlemarch</u>

The main reason for choosing this passage is for the
opportunities it offers to develop pupils' awareness
of point of view in prose extracts. They can either
read and discuss it on their own, with a few specific
questions to consider, or it can be considered during
a teacher directed class discussion.

In the previous passage about Mrs. Farrinder the
narrator focused upon one character. The narrator,
it was agreed, did not share Mrs. Farrinder's
opinion of herself; from the way he expressed his
impressions we were confident that he disliked her
and wanted his readers to share his view of her as
aggressive and overbearing. The author, therefore,
communicated a distinct impression of this particular
narrator. This passage also focuses upon a single
character, Dorothea, and her marriage prospects.
George Eliot, however, presents several opinions
about this, including Dorothea's. Like Henry James,
she, as author, lets us know what she thinks of the
people who hold these opinions. What we hope that
pupils will discover is that whilst the author is
informing us about what different people think about
her central character, she is also informing us about
them. To what extent is she approving or disapprov-
ing?

Because the 'content' is obvious from the
opening question and because we are mainly interested in viewpoint, the best approach to class discussion might be to discuss the extract in two broad
sections - conventional opinion of Dorothea and then
her view of herself - and to explore each paragraph
separately. To do so might strengthen pupils' sense
of how the development of the whole passage - from
the wary suitor to Dorothea's marital fantasies -
relates to the opening question about her marriage.
Each paragraph, moreover, raises the question of
how closely the author agrees with her characters'
opinions, of themselves and on other issues.

INTRODUCTION

It might be helpful, as a way of anticipating the
variety of viewpoints in this extract, to spend some
time on class discussion about describing people in
everyday life. The main point of this is to remind
pupils of the means we use to explain what people
are like, after having given straightforward information about age, appearance, financial and social
standing. Frequently, we report our own and other
people's opinion of someone we are describing,

especially if we are discussing a complicated
situation, like marriage or performance in a job. In
a discussion of this kind pupils readily recognise
the likelihood of differences of opinions and of
differences between those held by characters of themselves and by other people. They might be reminded,
at some point, of the additional information and
opinions likely to be present in novels, because of
the advantages the author has over the rest of us.
How many possibilities, in fact, are available? Not
only as many viewpoints on someone as the author
chooses to give, but the character's own opinion,
which also is in the control of the author. Because
pupils appear to find this question of viewpoint
difficult, it might be worth leading into it by one
or more of several routes: considering pupils' diversity of responses to someone; looking at their
responses to characters in literature which have
become well known to everyone; leading into a complex passage by way of a familiar piece of material
which attempts something similar; asking pupils to
prepare readings of this which communicate the
variety of perspectives in the passage.

Before reading this passage from Middlemarch it
will be necessary to explain to most groups 'like a
Papist' and its significance, as well as 'the
judicous Hooker' and 'John Milton in his blindness'.
To neglect these is to risk pupils missing the
humour of the contrast between these great figures
and Sir James and weaken their sense of George
Eliot's complicated attitude towards Dorothea.


CLASS DISCUSSION

First Section

After pupils have followed a public reading ask them
to reread the first paragraph and to consider,
firstly, the significance of the opening question.
Dorothea is marriageable and it is inconceivable
that she will not marry. And yet this question
raises doubts. In the light of any introductory discussion about describing and interpreting character
it will be agreed that this is a complex question
about any young woman, especially a handsome,
wealthy girl in conventional rural society. This
might be the point at which to map the whole passage
lightly. Either before the first public reading, or
at this point when we are asking for note taking,
small group discussion or class contributions,

pupils might find it helpful to be told that the
extract attempts to answer this opening question. We
are about to learn what different people think of
Dorothea and what George Eliot thinks of them.

Ask pupils to find out what discourages a likely
suitor about Dorothea's behaviour and why, according
to the author, it has this effect upon him - 'love of
extremes ... interfere with political economy and the
keeping of saddle horses'.

Looking closely at what George Eliot tells us
about him - 'wary', 'sane people did what their neighbours did' - how do we know that she does not completely share his view of Dorothea's love of extremes? What are we being invited to criticise him
for?

How does the introduction of 'rural opinion'
and the 'amiable and innocent-looking Celia' affect
our view of Dorothea and her suitor? Pupils who
have observed that conventional attitudes towards
women are partly responsible for Dorothea appearing
to be eccentric can be asked to consider why she
is described as 'Poor Dorothea' in comparison
with her sister. What might be the relationship
between the first paragraph's 'wary man' and the
repeated 'innocent-looking' Celia?

Similarly, why do men find Dorothea charming and
bewitching 'when she is on horseback', when 'she
looked very little like a devotee'?

## Second Section

Thus far, Dorothea has been described from the viewpoints of a cautious suitor, rural opinion and 'most
men' who admire her 'on horseback'. Pupils who have
been introduced to the organisation of this description and prepared for the variety of viewpoints have
observed that George Eliot has found ways of appealing over the heads of these characters for readers'
critical judgement of them.

Next pupils can be asked to look more closely
at Dorothea in the final paragraph to discover
how far the author is in agreement with the view
she holds  of herself. Is George Eliot appealing
to readers over her head as she has over the heads
of her admirers and critics? The final paragraph
is likely to present some difficulties for inexperienced readers. They may be helped by being given
a few moments to consider the last sentence of
the 'riding' paragraph as an introduction. What
is George Eliot's attitude towards Dorothea's

pleasure? How sensible is she to feel guilty about riding, and how do we know that it is the guilt and not the riding which the author thinks is the real indulgence?

Ask pupils to reread the last paragraph in the light of the opening compliments, especially 'not in the least self admiring'. Focus attention upon Dorothea's attitude towards Sir James; '... that he should be regarded as a suitor to herself would have seemed to her a ridiculous irrelevance'. How seriously does George Eliot intend us to take Dorothea's humility if she can so readily bestow upon her sister a suitor whom she finds inferior? How further does she contradict this opinion Dorothea holds of herself? Once pupils have spotted Dorothea's vanity and self deception they can move on to comment on the significance of her marital fantasies. What is likely to be George Eliot's view and, she hopes, ours, of a young girl who anticipates marriage as 'delightful' and where 'your husband was a sort of father'?

The topic, subject matter or content, therefore, is Dorothea's marriage prospects. The first part of the extract explores the views of conventional society and, as we have seen, undermines them in various ways. The second part explores Dorothea's views of herself and marriage and undermines these also by similar appeals to the reader. The author is sympathetic about the uncertainties surrounding Dorothea's prospects – 'Poor Dorothea' – partly because of society's narrowness and hypocrisy and partly because Dorothea is naive about herself and about what marriage is likely to mean.

It is hoped that most pupils will be able to comment upon two points: Dorothea's public advantages and private problems; and the inclusion of different people's viewpoints in the passage. If they can give an account of how the passage raises and answers a question, that is, how it moves from 'the wary man' and 'rural opinion' to 'those who approached Dorothea' and then to Dorothea herself, they will have shown that they are beginning to read the passage observantly. After a heavily directed class discussion along these lines, many teachers will probably wish to choose a similar passage or passages which describe characters from different points of view for pupils to explore by themselves. What is being suggested here is that, if they are becoming confident about the sorts of questions to consider, pupils can try, on their own, to identify the subject matter in prose extracts and to be observant about how writers have presented it.

BIBLIOGRAPHY

Adams, A. and Hopkin, T. Sixth Sense - Alternatives
    in Education 16-19 English: A Case Study
    (Blackie, London, 1980)
Brown, J. and Gifford, T. 'Creative Responses in
    the Sixth Form', English Studies, 11-18,
    edited by Bernard J. Harrison (Hodder and
    Stoughton, London 1983)
Coombes, H. Literature and Criticism (Chatto and
    Windus, London 1953)
D'Arcy, P. 'In Search of Style', Learning about
    Learning, Booklet No. 8
Druce, R. The Eye of Innocence (Brockhampton Press,
    London 1965)
Elmer, G. and Peim, N. 'Othello: A Drama Approach
    to 'A' level English', Drama and Dance, vol. 3,
    no. 3 (1984)
Ferrar, M. 'Linguistics and the Literary Text',
    The Use of English 35/2 (1984)
Gill, R. 'Poetry at Advanced level', The New
    Leicestershire Journal, Issue no. 7 (1983)
Ginger, J. An Approach to Criticism (Hodder and
    Stoughton, London 1970)
Gribble, J. Literary Education: a Revaluation
    (Cambridge University Press, 1983)
Harcourt, R. Sharing Literature (Oliver and Boyd,
    Edinburgh 1975)
Harrison, C. Readability in the Classroom
    (Cambridge University Press, 1980)
Holbrook, D. English for Meaning (NFER Windsor
    1979)
Hollingworth, B. 'Crisis in English Teaching' The
    Use of English 34/2 (1983)
Holmes, E. What Is and What Might Be (Constable,
    London, 1911)
Knight, R. 'Review' of Literary Text and Language
    Study, The Use of English 33/3, (1982)

'Practical Criticism Examined,', English in
    Education, vol. 17, no. 3 (1983)
Morris, R. Towards Reading Maturity (Penguin Books,
    Harmondsworth, 1973)
Milford, J. 'Comments on Traditions of Literature
    Teaching' Children as Readers (Schools Council,
    1973)
Mulhern, F. The Moment of Scrutiny (NLB, London,
    1979)
Peet, M. and Robinson, D. The Critical Examination
    (Pergamon Press, Oxford, 1977)
O'Brien, V. Teaching Shakespeare (Edward Arnold,
    London)
Read, H. Education through Art (Faber, London,
    1943)
Rosen, H. Language Study, the Teacher and the
    Learner (Edward Arnold, London, 1973)
Rosenblatt, L. Literature as Exploration (Heinemann,
    London, 1970)
Self, D. Critical and Creative (Harrap, London,
    1984)
Squire, J.R. and Applebee, R.K. Teaching English in
    the United Kingdom (USA National Council of
    Teachers of English, 1969)
Steiner, G. Language and Silence (Faber, London,
    1967)
Stenhouse, L. 'Open Minded Teaching' New Society,
    July 24, 1969
Strickland, G. Structuralism or Criticism
    (Cambridge University Press, 1981)
Suleiman, S. The Reader in the Text (Princeton
    University Press, Princeton, 1980)
Watson, G. The Discipline of English (The Macmillan
    Press, London, 1978)
Whitehead, F. 'Stunting the Growth. The Present
    State of English Teaching', The Use of English
    28/1 (1976)

# NAME INDEX

Abbs, Peter 12
Adams, Antony vii, 16
Anderson, Perry 7

Bantock, G.H. 32
Barnes, Douglas 42
Barstow, Stan 63, 69
Belsey, C. 47
Britton, James 35, 42

Coleridge, S.T. 35
Coombes, H. 28

D'Arcy, P. x, 66-67
Donne, John 61
Doughty, P. 11

Eagleton, T. 47, 65
Eliot, George 58
Eliot, T.S. 55, 59

Ferrar, M. 2-3
Ford, B. 16
Freeman, E.A. vii

Gill, R. 66-67
Golding, W. 63
Gribble, James viii

Harcourt, Roger 28-29
Hawkes, T. 47
Heaney, Seamus 37
Hobsbaum, P. 12
Holbrook, David 12, 35,
   36, 48
Hollingworth, B. 5, 46-47

Holmes, Edmond 36
Holt, J. 40
Hourd, Marjorie 35
Hughes, Ted 57-58, 62,
   69
Hughes, Richard 58

Inglis, Fred 11, 12, 32

Keats, John 60, 62
Keddie, Nell 40
Knight, Roger vii, 12,
   23-24

Lawrence, D.H. 5, 53-54,
   59-60, 62, 63, 69
Lawton, D. 42
Leavis, F.R. 6, 79, 32,
   46
Lodge, David 4

Marvell, Andrew 54-55,
   56, 57
McCabe, Colin 45
Mulford, Jeremy 9
Mulhern, Francis 6, 9,
   45-47

O'Brien, V. 64
Owen, Wilfred 55-56, 59

Peet, M. 14, 29
Postman, N. 40

Richards, I.A. x, 32-33
Read, Sir H. 36

Robinson, D. 14, 29
Rosen, Harold 42
Rosenblatt, Louise xiii

Sillitoe, Alan 63
Steiner, George 8, 44-45
Strickland, G. 7
Suleiman, S. x, xii

Thompson, Denys 32

Watson, G. 7
Whitehead, Frank 12, 48
Widdowson, P. 47
Wordsworth, William 35

Yeats, W.B. 60

Associated Examining
    Board vii, ix, 21, 23,
    25-27

background to poems and
    prose extracts 53,
    60-62
Bible 33, 44
Bullock Report 1

Cambridge English 6-9,
    12, 45, 47
Certificate of Secondary
    Education 36, 38, 51
Classics vii, 6, 33, 38,
    44
course books 14, 27-30
creative English 5, 33-37,
    39
creative writing viii, 10,
    37, 51-52, 69-70
critical terminology viii,
    xii, 22-25, 26-30, 37,
    50-51, 65

deconstructionist theories
    3, 4
drama 34, 42, 63-65

examinations vii-viii,
    17-21, 35, 50-51
examiners' reports 21-24,
    26

folder work 36, 68

grammar schools 14

Humanities 40-41, 48
Humanities Project 39

introductions to lessons
    52-62

linguistics ix, 2, 4,
    10-11, 33

Marxist theories 5, 46

'New Left' 40
Newsom Report 41
Northern Universities
    Joint Matriculation
    Board 19, 20, 22
note taking 65-69

oral work 5, 6, 4-43
organisation of poems
    and prose extracts
    56-59
Oxford and Cambridge
    Schools Examination
    Board 18

post structuralism 2, 3,
    32, 46

readability of literary
    material 59-60
reading aloud 51, 52,
    62-65

reader response theory ix-xi

Scrutiny 6, 45
Southern Universities
   Joint Board 19, 20
structuralism 2, 3, 30,
   46-47
stylistics ix, 2, 4,
   10-11, 33

themes 38, 46
Times Higher Education
   Supplement 1, 4
titles of poems 54-56

traditional grammar 33,
   43

University of Cambridge
   Examination Board
   20, 23-24
University of Cambridge
   Plain Text Examina-
   tion 36-37
University of London
   Examination Board
   18-19
Use of English 2, 4

Welsh Joint Education
   Committee 20, 25-26